I0528785

In Praise of
Within my Shadows, Into my Light

Here is a poet who has finally touched on the core of life – no billboard bombast – hers is organic genius that blooms and arches to heights few poets ever even dream of attaining, I am left speechless by her depth, width, scope, by her voice that seems to cull and weave into every verse, line the very essence of what it means to be human. What an amazing talent.

I've waited a long time for such a poet, her collection of poems draws on pain and joy of living and braids them both into an evocation of sublime beauty. She is undoubtedly the best young poet of her generation.

This book of poetry will become a classic-- its power issues from some sacred place in her body, where voice kindles with magic and both ignite to illuminate our human journey-- after reading hundreds of books and poems, I find one that leaves me in awe.

—**Jimmy Santiago Baca**, award-winning poet,
essayist, novelist, and executive producer/author
of the feature film, *Blood In, Blood Out*

Melina Martinez's *Within My Shadows, Into My Light* is that rare poetic voice that graces us with its profound maturity, written by a sharply acute and intelligent mind, flowing from her beautiful Latina heart.

Her work carries an intricate, subtle, yet direct constant affirmation of the strength required to love, to understand and to forgive, a universal message accessible to generations of readers.

This book, written with its natural, almost effortless brilliance, creates a poetic balance that is quietly majestic in its realism and its resounding faith in our hope and strength.

—**Antonio Salazar-Hobson**, author;
2023 Emmy Award for Crime/Social Issues;
17th Annual Indies Award, LatinX: Best Non-Fiction
for *Antonio, We Know You*

Within My Shadows, Into My Light is an emotionally raw, unpredictable journey deep into the human heart. Cascading through life's darkest moments and brightest epiphanies, the poems illustrate the power of words to make us feel and heal, exploring love and loss, faith and family, nature's bounty, and transformative self-exploration.

Martinez's words have the power to take us to unexpected places: a man in jail 'stripped to his essence, there isn't even a belt loop on which to loop his thumbs;' a desperate Catholic sleeping in Church pews 'hoping to encounter Jesus, a being I could trust with my suffering'; a smitten fifteen year old experiencing a brutal betrayal when 'not knowing what sex meant, into the car she went.'

The collection is an achingly tender, soul-churning voyage as paradoxical as life itself—excruciatingly heartbreaking, whimsically joyous, and astoundingly enlightening. For as the author says, "What is hell, but the shadow of heaven?"

—**Hida Viloria**, author of
Born Both: An Intersex Life Human Rights Activist

Melina Martinez's poetry is a new day's sun rising on the horizon. Her words blossom at me when the world needs it the most. Her work is transcendent and has the power to comfort—like a warm blanket made of words that swaddles us on a cold crisp night and makes us feel we are not alone, but mostly, her words soar above the discord and noise and serve to remind us that we are all human.

Her poetry is sad, humorous, painful, beautiful, impactful, and honest. Melina's poetic fire stokes souls and binds us all through a sensorial journey. This book is a herald of hope. Get lost in her words. Rediscover the beauty of Humanity. Be entranced by Melina.

—**Manny Rey**, author of
In the Name of the Father, the Son, and Everything Raza
and *El Chuco: Chicano Poems That are Chido*

Within my Shadows, Into my Light

FLOWERSONG
PRESS

poetry by
Dr. Melina Martinez

FLOWERSONG
PRESS

FlowerSong Press
Copyright © 2023 by Melina Lujan Martinez
ISBN: 978-1-953447-14-2

Published by FlowerSong Press
in the United States of America.
www.flowersongpress.com

Cover Art by James Drake
Cover Design by Priscilla Celina Suarez
Author Photo Credit: Lonnie Anderson
Set in Adobe Garamond Pro

No part of this book may be reproduced without
written permission from the Publisher.

All inquiries and permission requests should
be addressed to the Publisher.

NOTICE: SCHOOLS AND BUSINESSES
FlowerSong Press offers copies of this book at quantity discount with
bulk purchase for educational, business, or sales promotional use. For
information, please email the Publisher at info@flowersongpress.com.

Acknowledgments

A special thank you to my children and wonderful husband who have supported me in my writing with big cheers, hugs, cups of coffee, warm blankets and lots of love. Thank you for believing in me and my passion to share parts of myself which could only be shared through writing.

Thank you to my mother, father and brothers for being the strength from which I was born and loving me enough to give me the fortitude to follow my passions.

Dr. Alexander Paret, thank you for teaching and guiding me gently and purposefully through the importance of finding meaning, pursuing passions, and working through my faulty thinking to find the beauty and poetry which has always been inside me.

Special gratitude to Jimmy Santiago Baca who heard my voice and never stopped encouraging me to write and insisted that I needed to have my book published. Thank you for illuminating my path and helping me embrace my own wonderful weirdness.

Thank you James Drake for reading my book and being so excited to create the brilliant original art for my cover which couldn't be more perfect! Thank you Lonnie Anderson for taking my photo in the middle of chemotherapy and making it look like me. Thank you FlowerSong Press and Edward Vidaurre for believing in my work and saying yes!

And lastly, thank you to music, paintings, sculptures, books, science, food, coffee, my beautiful mountains, nature, my furry companions and all the beautiful people who continually bless me with their existence, always giving me inspiration to continue evolving.

table of contents

For Avah, Augustine, Ernest
and
all those who have ever struggled with life.

Within my Shadows, Into my Light

Shadows

The light is tinted red,
however,
there is something so beautiful I can see
between heaven and me

What is hell,
but the shadow of heaven?

I love with the same trepidation
that I love my own unruly darkness

There is no equality
outside my heart

I love the light I can see
flickering through the holes in the wall,
it's what continues to ail me

To the Elder(s)

Idealistic fools needn't be anything else.

Idealistic fools,
    the world will eat you up,
             devour you!!!

Well it did.
    You were right.

However,
    when I tried to be someone else,
      I never could.

So who am I now?
        Me.

Idealistic.
      A fool.
  And it's worth it.

Idealists fools,
    the world needs us.

So please,
    just be.

And yes,
    you were right to be worried.

There were times I almost didn't make it.

And now I can see,
      there will be more moments like this.

But I'm here today,
        and I'm smiling.

Because I still believe in good.
        I still believe in kindness.
    I still believe in trust.

I still believe in love.

And if this is how I die,
      because I was too idealistic.

And if evil comes to feast upon my flesh.

Please applaud me,
      for I was finally true to myself.

An idealistic fool.

Scatter Me

When I die sneak my ashes to the top of Atalaya

……..even if the landscape has been transformed and all the trees
have burned,
Please scatter me slowly and deliberately

…………..For my love for the mountain isn't dependent on her
trees or greenery
I do not love her for the shade she provides

I love her for her ever changing landscape,
        and especially for her ability to persist in new and different ways

No, my love isn't dependent on any semblance of permanence,
        nor timeliness

It is however attached to a certain longitude and latitude that always
feels like home

If my ashes are to find more ashes, let us become one

And if they are to find a forest in full bloom,
        I will be quite content to feed the latest growth

Shall you come upon a new home emerging from the ground,
            allow me to become part of the foundation where children
might play
or lovers might lay

        Believe me when I say, I am un-phased by the mountain's
circumstance

The truth is,
  I am deeply drawn to the rising slopes that reach out to the heavens

 I am captivated by her evolution

And my favorite place of all,
    is to meld with the horizon
   where earth and sky combine to gaze upon it all

Fly on the Wall

I love the way people give one another
…….particles of the air they have breathed
……………of the lives they have lived
little fragments of who they are
…….and what makes them feel
And I like the way it makes me feel
…..when I see the smiles
………when I hear the voices soak into it all
…Oh how it makes my little heart sing

Husband

We fell in love playing in the streams
Casting hopes and dreams up to the stars
Cool rain falling tenderly on our skin
Ushering us to speak of all that stirred within
You warmed me with your giving spirit
Seedlings of love planted in my soul
We walked all through the night
With the universe stitching our hearts as one
You were golden in the sunshine
Eyes sparkling sweet intellect
Sunrise to sunset
Inseparable then, inseparable now
We are joined by the hands of God for this sacred journey
You stand before me today
As noble as any King I've ever dreamt
No other stands so tall
You walk the mile
Blistered feet
Your heart, it does not cease
You are an anchor of all that seeks the light
Your strength is a pillar built on stone
Holding up all that rises to the sky
Your kindness is a flower
Unfolding in the morning sun
Your love is the radiant sky
Morning and night
Your brilliance is the water
Giving nourishment when days go dry

My wish for you
Endless love of family
Flowing freely like a stream
Sweet melodies
Painting your hours
Coloring your minutes
I wish you the gift of laughter
Coating you down with sweetness
From the inside to the outside
Let kindness be the scents
Surrounding you in the forest
Which linger in the air
After the rain does fall
Please do hear my souls song for you
It comes from deep within
I love you

Ode to hand

A hand reached down to grab me
from where I was drowning
deep inside my heart

It pulled me up
to see the sky
rather than the deep blue
water covering my head

I had grown so tired
of my saturated breaths

So I felt myself
being yanked out from my own sea
then I saw the sky again

Now I lay on the shore soaking wet
somehow in the absence of people
but no longer alone

Vanity

There she was beside me
......and my cheeks were roses just for her
......my skin, the porcelain vase to house
I was her most beautiful child
.......I was pure, I was clean
.......I was all that was taken from within
She dressed me in white
.......and weaved flowers into my hair
My pedestal was lined with gold
My house, six walls of glass
.......quieting my sounds
.......never to let out
And the people walking by
........clicked photos one by one
You can still find my images
........hung upon some walls
And you may still find me
.................smiling at the lens
Regardless of the gashes on my neck
.......the stains upon my dress
Secretly
...hoping to be pretty
.....wanting to be pretty
.........dying to be pretty

Right off the shelf

Are you really satisfied
in your button up shirt
and picture perfect life?
Can't you see
that you still want,
regardless
Constantly trying to tame your appetite
wanting one singular dance
just so you can have another
on a different day
Constantly trying to quench your thirst
in moderation of course,
so that you can keep having more
over and over
in ways that you are allowed
So clean and neat
like whiskey
in a pretty glass
All straight lines.......
....
This is the new age me
the Version 2.0 excel,
excel for excelente
The one who colors between the lines
so that I can continue being me
on another day
by the same name
I'm upgraded
I now possess all the bells and whistles
I shine like a sparkly new iPhone

I no longer want because I have
I'm now satisfied
I have it all figured out
No more glitches
Fresh out the box!

Love's Regard

Have you ever loved
How did it taste
Did it have a color
Did it have a sound
How did it feel against your skin
Did you feel it in your breath
Did it make you laugh
as you sat quietly under a tree
or cry in the shower
with water trickling down your face
Did you notice it in your thoughts
as you awoke at 2 AM
overcome with emotion
Did you feel elated
as you closed your eyes
and looked at the images
impressed upon your heart
Did this love make you want to be better
than any version of yourself you had ever met
And did it make you willing
to put yourself away
tucked up on the shelf
so that you could quietly add
and never subtract from the happiness in your sight
Did this love make you want
anything in the world for that person
even if it took them away from you
Did it lead you to walking on the edge
of where a mountain touches the sky
balancing carefully on the horizon
being careful as to not fall off the slim edge…

And at the end of the day
Did it make you glad that it came into your life
even if it left you breathless and powerless
in complete surrender of whatever
that particular loved begged for
Did it leave you kindly obliging to its needs...
Sometimes just a few drops
are the concentrate
with which all flavors are made....
One lovely, beautiful, gorgeous drop
It's enough to carry you through the
the empty corridors that are sometimes life

Pushing Up Daisies

Ohh, I must be dreaming
I'm six feet under
My momma dropped a flower in my grave
Only, she doesn't know I'm not really there
That's why it was a closed casket
Locked tight, even in my death
Such irony,
I was actually cremated
Taken to the Truchas Peaks,
Given to the wind to take me home
The home I so longed for

My brothers said I was a fool
Trying to amount to something
When I was really just spinning my wheels
They feared they were just like me
They loved me, yet they hated me
Because I had a vagina
Because momma could
Never really stand a penis
Even when it belonged to her own son

This was my cross as well,
The one between my legs…

Everyone was laughing at the funeral
Remembering how I wanted to pee standing up
Me and Freud thought it was funny too
I was in the backyard with the boys when I was six
Checking all my pockets for my dick
I guess I thought if I could whip it out

Then maybe daddy could love me
Maybe he could remember my name
He died last year, in my house, in my arms,
Now he knows my name

I heard my husband asking the *Hermanos*,
His brothers on their knees
To pray for me
I don't think he believes
I will ever make it to heaven
He knows my sins so well
Most of them were against him
Yet he loves me for being a good mom
For changing my ways
And he loves me
For some value I simply can't see
At the same time he hates me
For all my bad
Yet somehow,
He manages to extinguish
The flames in his eyes
And have love for me
I love him for that
He is so confused by me
And He may always be

My children, they loved me
They know I would have died for them
In fact they know I actually did die for them
This was a long time ago
This isn't all that bad
Some parts of me that died,
Were vile and putrid
Some of the same parts
Were deeply acquainted with God
I had to let go of them all
So my children could continue to breath
Through my own breath

Many people think I was a coward
Especially those I walked away from
They couldn't understand why I would stay
In a marriage that covered me in dirt

What they didn't know
Was the dirt was all mine
What they didn't know
Was I was brave for getting my shovel
To dig my way out every single day
For digging out a hole from which to breath

What they also failed to see
Is that flowers grow from dirt
And I grew flowers
Many many flowers

Supermarket Flowers for Mom

This is for you Dearest Mom, giver of life
Light has begun to shine upon the dark recesses of my thoughts
the areas where the doors had been kept shut
I am so grateful that you still breath air as I do
for it is time I slow my pace, look around and notice
that the things from which I flee, they are the very things
which will destroy me if I keep running
I must be brave and come to a standstill, look you in the eyes,
hold your gaze, be not afraid to cry, be not afraid crumble
I will take my strength from you dear Mom
I will be brave enough to own what you have given me
I will no longer be unworthy due to my weakened heart
for I have been fortified by all that is good in you
I will no longer lean on the things which hurt me
It is the walk of the tired and defeated
My shoulders shall not be slumped in the face of my failures
I will lift my head from my deepest shame
It is time I bravely claim what I am capable of being in the light
Claim what you planted inside of me all those years ago
You were my Angel, knowing the things I would come to need in time
You delivered them with abundance never tiring of seeing the good in me
hoping someday it would be enough to see me through my own darkness
Well its time you know, it was enough, it was enough to sprout new life
after I caused so much destruction,
It was enough to find goodness in myself
when I thought I had burnt all my virtue to ashes
Mom, your love HAS seen me through
so I will stop my running and slow my pace
I will come inside and sit across the table from you
I will pour us a cup of coffee, I will pour us a glass of wine
and with you in my sight, I will be brave enough to remember

the magnitude of all the love you have given me
I will sip with you, laugh and talk about life
I will never look away again
I will accept the tears that are to come
from opening my heart to the truth of your love

Fire in Her Eyes

What she endured was wrong, and she knew it.......

Mariana is life
She is indestructible, defiant of the crowd

The world told her no, it told her die
she refused!

Her eyes are life, they are fire
never defeated, never a quitter
In her shadow, I witness
she is strength

They say men don't cry
Mariana's eyes are always dry
in the church with loved ones gone
there are memories of life
and her faith in death
no tears on her face

When the nightmares came
I've heard her scream
I've seen the terror in the night
sweat resembling blood
and so she fights for her life
like it's so much more than hers alone

When the clock turns time
and the earth keeps spinning
It's all the same, in one gasp of breath

They tell her its time for her to go
And her body starts to fail
her bones crush under the weight
her skin tears like a ripened peach

In her soul is more fight
her eyes are of a warrior
they are bright and dark in unison
deeper than the darkest sky
with stars just as same

She always fights
she tries to do what's right
she keeps getting up
with a sword strapped to her back

The angels sing for her
the Heavens open up
she is serenaded by the glorious
by the clean, by the pure
trumpets, a harp, the voice of God
She asks not for herself
for she knows how to love
as well as she knows hate

She refused to die
she could barely speak
she hardly had the strength
and her tears did not fall
just prayers to the wind

She told them NO
rage and fire in her eyes
like a boiling cup of coffee
no sugar, no milk,
Black
full of caffeine
shining hotly

She believes
siting on salvation's doorstep
all the wrongs will turn to right
And I believe
her flame will never die
I refuse

Lost innocence

Frigid winter
. . . .
She just celebrated her 15th birthday
beautiful child, dreaming of the stars
Christmas Pageant and biscochitos
3 Wise Men, Silent Night and Catholic kids
For the first time she had just tasted another's lips
She was swooning from the flavor of the night
She was in love, dreaming of being held tight
A girl not knowing what sex meant, into the car she went
Her boyfriend and girlfriends
sheltered her from the mounting snow
Out came a gun, aimed straight at her head
Her trusted friends, escaping the moving car,
rolling onto the icy ground
Not her, she was right between too many legs
the warmest spot for the most favored
Four perpetrators,
the boy she loved and his kid brother
the third, a local boy
and the fourth was the devil himself
At gunpoint she was driven amongst the pinion trees
the Devil was the first to beat her with his gun, with his fist
He shoved the gun in her vagina, his penis
He raped her with a smile, with laughter
She fought, she kicked, she scratched, she bit
and when he was finished
She spit at him and vowed him to burn in hell
He made the other three beat her and rape her at gun point
They broke everything but her hatred,
Her ripped flesh tied to a tree

24

Her crimson blood painted demons in the snow
But what hurt the most, was the boy she loved, he didn't save her
He beat her, he raped her with tears in his eyes and a hard dick
as the devil called him names.............
....
She heard voices talking about where they would dispose of her
Wondering how long it would be for her to die
wondering if they should put a bullet in her head
It was so cold, below zero that night
All got quiet........
deathly quiet, the snow had stopped, the clouds cleared
She could barely open her eyes
above were the most beautiful stars she had ever seen
There she searched for God
but she couldn't find Jesus, no Virgin Mary, no Angels, no Saints
There was no one there,
...........just stars, planets and the moonlight
Then she heard it, a voice say RUN
RUN as a whisper in her ear, a scream to her soul
She unraveled her ties
She ran, ran, and ran into the night,
with savage men on her heals
cruel words in her ears
Cold, exhausted, lost, and quiet once again
she collided with the barbed wire fence
It cut her back to life, she was lost no more
It was the cemetery near her village
where the dead were lying in wait to lead her home
She escaped with her life and a heart full of hatred
She made it to the sheriff, the doctor
Her brother drove her, bloodied and beaten
All evidence present, collected, photos taken
A search was issued
The oldest in his twenties
the others teenagers.....
All were captured in a different states
The prosecutor was her only friend,
not even her mom was on her side

Her mother's voice faded into silence
everyone fell away, like leaves in the fall
She took all 4 to trial, unheard of in her town
Rape was hardly a crime, and women weren't worth much
She fought, ostracized by her community, by her family
Her father accepted money to have her drop the case
Begging and pleading, he said she would never win
She refused, and her father gave the money back
and turned his back further against his daddy's girl
She was the smart one, the strong one, the prettiest of all
and now she was the dirty one, the worthless one
all used up, no longer an asset to the family
Death threats mounted, rocks shattered windows
She was now the town puta
Abuse escalated, her public trial marching on
....
She won, she WON in the fifties, setting a precedent in NM
The Devil himself got a life sentence
The other 3 would still never see the light of day in their youth
With this, she left town
The boy who was her first love
wrote her daily, begging for her forgiveness
She couldn't, she wasn't ready
So the boy hung himself one hopeless day
and the name murderer was added to her name..........
————
For all People who have endured horrendous crimes
-with all my love

February Snow

Winter so frigid
snow turned to sandpaper
wind blowing to a sting
teasing the sun into play
hints of green peeking through
promising new beginnings

Against all odds a new life persists
for Father to be had been pruned to a fruitless tree

Timing was twisted,
but for the child's hand alone

The Deck was shuffled
lit with a match, flame ignited
given oxygen with thy mother's breath
like a wooden bellow and its gentle puff

Flames grew taller, burning with no regard
for the rules of the game
wild yet contained in her mother's softly lined pit

Fire was tended
sheltered from the cold blowing Northern Winds
by a mother's dreams, brighter than the Sun
She refused to crumble under the weight of the truth
and the lies that never were

She was a Coat of Arms
till accusations collapsed

under medical mysteries no more
and so the child was born

Alas, she was her father's daughter
through and through

Circus

There once was this man
He was intelligent and kind
He was quiet
He was loud
It just depended on his crowd
I asked him about his dreams
He said he would love to join the circus
Maybe the carnival
Buy a food cart
Sell all the greatest snacks
The first time I heard it
I chuckled, thinking it a joke
It just couldn't be
So I scratched my head and spoke
You could be a doctor a lawyer
A great entrepreneur or grand philosopher
You could create such wealth, stability, a legacy

He said he didn't need money
Or a house
Just enough to eat
A place to lay his head
How would you not worry, I begged
God, he said
What was the appeal I inquired
He looked off into the distance.......
No Past, No future
Just today he smiled
This was Father
Never before did I hear
Something so beautiful
So sad

Story of a Boy

Like most little girls, dad was my hero.
He a strange creature raising himself on the streets.
Abandoned by his mother, given away like an unwanted puppy,
because his hair was golden and not brown like it was supposed to be.

His mother died when he was seven,
He was passed around till his father died when he was 11.
By that point, he knew how to fish, hunt and live off the generous land.

Taken to the orphanage at age eleven,
He refused to be tamed by the nuns
who thought only corporal punishment could tame such an unruly child.

He told stories of eating out of dumpsters,
hopping trains and fishing the canals of Arizona when he was just 12.
He read the dictionary from cover to cover, it was his only salvation,
That and the kindness of the homeless people he encountered.

This man was incredible, intelligent, hard working, kind,
and as handsome as they come.

Educated on the streets,
He forged documents and joined the military at 14,
he always bragged about this.
In fact, when he recently passed away,
I found his army certificate that proves his age
when he finished basic training,
he carried it in his wallet all his life!

This man went on to be an accountant, loan shark, entrepreneur,
but found his home in the junkyards dotting the desert landscape.

It was amongst old junk cars,
and piles of rubble and rust that he felt most at home.

This man was really quite beautiful,
and who was I to ever complain because
he didn't know how to love me.
How could I not see the pain of his lifetime written all over him.
How could I not see the beauty in his bravery
to find the light in his darkened life?

I loved him madly,
but he had almost nothing for me,
and I could never blame him.
I couldn't blame him
when he was never there for me.
I couldn't blame him
when I learned that he had multiple lovers
and secret families.
I couldn't blame him
when my brothers and I found a chest of photos
that showed him with his other children and wife.

He lived a lifetime of lies.
And his last days were spent with me,
caring for him, not knowing how to love him best,
with so much silence between us.
I wanted to save him and show him ultimate love.
I got my wish in the end, at least part of it.
I held my father in my arms for the first and only time
as he gasped his last breath, and crossed over to the other side.

I helped him die, it's all I was ever capable of doing for him,
and him for me.

Nature vs. Nurture

When I was a young girl of about 10, I would write these poems of love and loneliness and one time I ventured to share one with my father in an attempt to get what I needed. What he nor anyone knew is I had already acquired issues from sources outside my parents, issues like abuse and rape. And so I bravely recited one of my originals with excitement and fear:

"I sit alone with my buckets of love,
....................filled to the brink,
with no one to share them with,
..............and nothing to water,
I have so much to give,
...............but nowhere to go,
I am alone, hoping for flowers to water..."

This is the only time I ever saw my father's eyes tear up. Not when loved ones passed, not when he was facing death in a hospital bed, or when my mom threw out all his belongings and his beloved dog and changed the locks. No, it was this time alone that I saw tears. And oddly enough he didn't seem to see me at all. All I could surmise is that somehow I was reflecting back to him the pain that was the child in HIM, the pain that I had inherited from him. Nature or nurture, this was most certainly both!

Orange Jumpsuit

It's amazing what a person might witness
when entering a jailhouse
armed with unconditional love
What can be witnessed is a whole new level of truth
the truth of what a human being looks like
when he has nothing left
A man in jail is a man stripped to his essence
There isn't even a belt on which to loop his thumbs
on which to anchor his value
The Pendalton shirt with the pearl snaps is gone
just like bank accounts, fancy vehicles and friends
Sometimes even sons, daughters, wives, and lovers
they all vanish
and so does pride and self-esteem
And with all these things separated from a man
the truth hangs heavily in the silence
and true identities are revealed
A person might witness something
some people would never believe
Like the naked nature of someone's heart
and if he is comprised more of love than hate
You might witness remorse
Underneath all the apologies and lack of apologies
You might understand strength
when another human being allows
the spit to be wiped from his face
and if you arrive with love,
you might be lucky to learn
if the man behind the bars
really did do the best that he could do
I was very lucky to learn

My side of the story

I'm the one that bailed him out
    I used my scholarship money
I was 18

Everyone had their opinions
   perhaps they were there,
   perhaps they had seen more than I

Maybe they saw the face of the other women smile after mom had
cut his hair, trimmed his beard and made him look dapper,
    or maybe they heard him and the other woman fucking in the
hotel room when they went to call him for dinner,
     possibly they even saw mom with bruises and had to untie the
ropes from her hands

    Perhaps they saw and heard none of it or all of it,
however, quite possibly,
    they knew what was true and what was not

But not me, I knew none of it first hand, witnessed nothing,
   I was never a fly on the wall. I was just a bank full of fowl words,
 a place where hatred was deposited

I didn't know much, other than everyone's anger
        seemed to run deeper than the Rio Grande Gorge,
and their lips were glued shut about certain events

The opinions were plentiful

    Me, I couldn't afford to have an opinion
because I knew I would love them either way,

both of them

My only job seemed to be to love
    to absorb their pain
        to feel one's shame
            the other's hatred

I won't' lie,
it was much easier for me to identify with shame rather than hate,
    so against all advice,
I drove across the state and learned about bail bondsmen
                                and the color orange

When I first saw the bars through the camera
and his shackled wrists,
        I felt it
the smallness inside him was ginormous

He used to be prideful
        boast about his strength
his intelligence,
        And it was true
I had seen moments when he was brighter than the Sun

But this day was different,
    It was so sad, heartbreaking
he looked so different behind the bars

He had shrunk,
    now frail
now weak
but he wasn't angry
        he wasn't full of hatred
Only shame
    to be seen like this
helpless, choice less

He always told me "we always have a choice"

And on this day,
the words he lived by burned him to the core,
they singed his very soul
This I witnessed, first hand

My brothers told me to leave him there
let him think of what he did

If they had seen his sunken face
        his posture,
if they had felt his remorse in the room like I had,
    they would know, no one needed to make him pay
He was paying with his pride, his freedom,
                        he paid with his integrity

It was one thing for him to be sitting there all alone
        it was clearly something else to have to face his daughter
    The one who admired him,
the one who clearly loved him unconditionally

And when we looked at one another,
        I felt his shame trickle to our toes
and it sat there like a puddle of my own urine,
                and in that moment I became as broken as he

His loneliness overcame me

People might swear he never felt remorse,
I know differently, I know the truth
because sometimes the truth
    lies in the space between two souls
witnessing each each other with open eyes,
and the truth was in the room that day
        where words were barely spoken

A Visit From Dad

In the stillness of the morning
scattered stars peek out the fleecy sky
Clouds feel like a blanket of wool
creating for me a warm embrace
Wrapped in cloud's softness
my breath is dampened
Warmth spreads over me
just enough fluorescence
gathered from the stars
forges my path through the dark

Oh my dear father,
this morning spoke loudly of you
I felt your joy in seeing my colossal pups
sniffing and running gracefully in the dark
I felt your gypsy soul make a stop just for me
and I remembered the character of your heart
Noticing how you visited the cathedral with no walls
in every rotation of the earth
You worshiped trees and stones in their every form
exalted in the glory of the dusty land and water that flowed
Your congregation was all in diversity of substance and flesh

In supplication
I couldn't help but ask for your love
remembering the way your heart would beat
with little nostalgia or thoughts of tomorrow
the past just a blurry mirage
Your memories existing
as if in a sack filled with pebbles and leaves,
tethered upon a stick
where you hoped to one day cast them out to sea

In this place of no past, no future
you loved in abundance and rarity of men
as your love was not intertwined with time
It stood firmly in an arena all its own
It was honest, clean and pure
It was that or nothing at all

Called by your wandering spirit
you roamed the earth from land to land
depositing and withdrawing in perfect balance
barely a trace of your footprints, for you carried so little
However, you possessed one precious gift that I hoped for
I was never quite large enough to ask, but my heart did ask
and my heart's request was not silent upon you

Dear Father,
you gave me the greatest gift you ever held
it was your life, it was your death
it was the moment in time to erase all doubt
The moment that was capable of encompassing all that I ever missed
I am so honored, I am so humbled, and I am so sorry
for ever being so small as to not hear you
The pulse of your being is no mistake
Thank you for knowing me so well
Thank you for your gift of incredible consequence
your love has been irreversibly received
your visit today was timely
and my gratitude shall give you wings

Barren Landscape

I remember well
working hard in the desert,
lifting waste from what once was
with my youthful hands and delicate back,
making myself strong
Even engine parts, heavily weighted are no match for my will,
packing scrap iron into junked cars
Torn leather gloves, grease stained fingerprints
working at gaining my father's love and approval
Wanting to be the hero that saves the day,
or at least saves my mother from the icy cold winters
I offer my father a bandaid for his apparent broken heart
which was broken long before I took this existence
I work for the love of a boy,
thinking he will give me the strength I need
to fulfill my desires of saving the day…….
………………………………………..
It's lonely out in the desert, the sun shines hotly,
toasting my skin into a nice golden brown
like the crusts of bread in the oven
I feel the grime beneath my nails, hydraulic oil,
gasoline, grease, everything toxic to humans I am covered in
The pretty red-pink transmission fluid runs over my skin
and I remember my pink bedroom
Toxic, toxic waste on my skin, toxic relationships all around
I am the mitigator, reducing damages…….
………………..…………
I work till I can't walk up a hill
I work till my body aches, and I work from sun up to sundown,
using my body and not my brain
Mindless work in a sense, making me so aware of myself

Wanting love, working for love
Painful, so painful that it becomes easy to get lost in the sunshine,
In the red mesas expanding before my eyes.........
....
An old lone tree twisted and now turned grey
casting its shadow on the ground,
creating a sanctuary for the small bugs,
for me

Intelligent Universe

God knew what he was doing when he made your eyes
sparkle like the sun.

The river knew what she was doing when her cool water
splashed upon your face.

The sky knew what it was conspiring when we looked up from the moist grass,
as the clouds rolled in and blessed our fate with the sweetest raindrops.

When my body was broken and in despair,
crying more tears of pain than I ever thought were possible,
the world knew I needed You, and no one else by my side.

When the warm Tahitian waters washed upon our feet
and we listened to the rhythm of the sea,
as we dined and laughed,
I knew the airplane had it right, to land us on the tiniest speck of land.

When we say our prayers at night,
I know your mom knew what she had to do, so that on exactly the
right night, I could see
the most spectacular father on the planet.

When I was so weak and turning to dust, lost in a cloudy haze of
confusion, not wanting to continue, Sun Mountain stepped up to
her destiny and showed us your strength that lay in wait
for the day that had come.

You my dear, knew what you were doing,
when you decided it was time to give our love a chance.

I am so blessed that you are the one that I get to stand beside
as we find our way on this discovery mission of life.

Today I am blessed that the very trees, sun, moon and earth have
been looking out for me,
so that we may meet once again to take one another's hand
and listen to the music played uniquely for You and Me.

I love you deeply, now more than ever, because I can see what the
Universe has done for me,
so that I can experience You.
You my dear, are amazing!

Coloring

Help me color inside the lines
let me be satisfied
with the subtleties that lie
within the borders that define
that outline
the differences between
right and wrong
let me be strong
enough to resist
all the temptations that exist
this world
it calls me
it wants me to taste
it begs for me
to let the paint brush fly
up and down
and deep within
places that are wild and free
no borders or lines
that confine

Rio Pueblo

Waiting for the heat of day
a child at play
Sandcastles built upon the sand
within the island of the river
Warming up in the sun
wanting to swim in her waters
Treasures collected
lined atop the riverbank
Waiting for that special hour
skipping stones and fishing poles
Waiting for that perfect moment
lemonade and finger sandwiches
Waiting for the guests of honor
holding back, patiently waiting
not wanting them to miss a thing
Perfect planning
.......some children will never again wait
they learn to jump right in
with or without you

Swirling

I'm swirling
Quiet down, close my eyes
Reopen them to an image
Image is a flavor, a color, a texture
Little particles in the atmosphere
Wishing to come in union with me
Me wanting to break apart
Into fragments of myself
Deconstruct and find myself
Scattered across many worlds
Particles of me
Mingled with particles of you
And him and her
We are all one
I long for it
I want to discard my individuality
I want to liquify and seep into the earth
Flow through the crevices till I reach water
Become one with the sea
Evaporate and become a cloud
Fly the greatest heights
Soar without tire
Till I am far from me
And then melt into my form
Newly invented of my original self
I have died and risen from the dead
My ashes have painted
A mural on the red sandstone
A mural telling the tale

A tale of a lifecycle of love and flight
I deposit myself along the shore
Deposit myself into others
....
.....

Inside the Box

I inch closer to the one who's brain is a brain
It thinks and categorizes
it feels within parameters
How? How?
Is this really what I want to be?
Am I even capable of this?
Is it the answer I seek?
I have bought and paid for the storyline
it had hefty price tag
I wish I could forget
I resigned myself into this box
Where what I feel is absolute
unwavering,
but limited
How I detest limits
and how I strive to perfect
my understanding of the inside of the box
See the exponential space
as it backs itself into nothing
less than nothing
I cannot argue it
till I know it
inside and out

Glass Animal(s)

Let's not anneal me.....
Temper me like glass,
why won't we?
Stop me from shattering,
and cutting
like jagged shards
that harm.
Clean me up and
sand away the roughness.
Run me through the oven.
Heat me up
to just before combustion.
Then quench me with
something ice cold,
so that when I break
I do so in an orderly,
organized,
crumbling way.
Somewhat harmless,
That's what we say.
You know, I can go up in flames.
like a match to paper,
I burn so hot and furious,
uncontainable,
unobtainable.
Squirming through your fingers,
wanting to be held.
No stopping till I'm ashes.
Then I rise again
like the bird that I claim.

Still a Child

I seek and seek, never ceasing
        I have an insatiable appetite for love
  To give and to receive.
Its somehow never enough for me
        leaving me feeling defective,
like there is something in this life I'm just not getting.
      Something my intellect can't grasp.
I try to manipulate the world into validating me,
      for deep down I can never be enough.
          Self imposed misery.
I know what the answer ought to be.
      Love myself, because validation from without
  will never be enough to quench my thirst.
I have so much,
      more than I could have dreamt about
in the meager beginnings of my life.
         My list is a mile long.
For I know how to manifest
  and achieve in most worldly ways.
  But because happiness eludes me,
I scrape the bottom of the barrel
    looking for answers,
and I don't know how to win,
      for I cannot win my own heart.

The Other Side of Truth

The smell of crisp air on a clear February morning. It's coldness pierces my skin and I'm reminded how my heart was dissected in an attempt to uncover some greater truth.

There is no greater truth than seeing the other side of truth, to commune with the Gods, to return and live out one's life with courage and purpose, walking on new lands and knowing what it is to love at the most difficult of times.

It is one thing to love when it is easy and effortless, yet perhaps the most truthful thing is to love when the ease of love has long been dead.

To love when the feeling is gone, to resurrect love after it has been pulverized and turned to dust.

It is truthful and painful to look in the mirror and notice your cold image devoid of color and attempt to think your way back to love.

The trail is laden with all the scars of a lifetime, but even more, it is covered with the present bittersweet cacophony of emotions and thoughts.

Exteriors tell so little of the story.

At times I struggle to avoid paralysis of the heart, I want to love, love what is easy and get lost in it till I regain my heart.

When You Don't Love Yourself

When you don't love yourself
you are always searching for it.
You may not even know it,
But every minute of your life,
somehow seems to be devoted to this quest.
You look for it in a song,
In the sky,
In a tree,
On a moonlit walk,
In the face of your family,
On the backs of friends,
In the words of a stranger.
You look in animals.
You look in interactions of the world,
Perhaps the way light falls across the land,
Or in the shadows of time.
You look in movies and in church.
You search in the dead and in the living.
You look in saints and in serial killers.
You turn over stones,
And study the particles of their structure.
Perhaps there is a clue
in the smoothness of a river rock,
Or the answer is in the crystals
that sparkle like snow.
You look to the ground,
as your footsteps fall upon a sandy beach.
Or in the waves, as they crash gently
upon the shore.

You listen for it in the soft breeze,
In a birds happy song,
Or in the lament of the howling wind.
You feel for this love in your body.
In the rhythm of your beating heart.
In your legs as you make them burn
carrying you desperately up a hill.
You search on a piece of paper,
 as words are formed or faces emerge.
You look for it everywhere.

Many of you may never understand this,
But some of you might.
You look deep into your childhood,
And all through out the moments of your life,
And it can elude us.
We solve puzzles, and do math,
Study physics and chemistry.
We turn over the pages of a history book
or classic literature.
We wonder where it went.
Why is it not present?
Was it stolen from us
or was it never there?
Is it something we deserve?
Or do we have to earn it
by forging the fires of hell?
Will it at long last be ours when we
finally walk through the gates of heaven?
Maybe we can feel it if we can meet Jesus.
Or if Father Sun sprouts legs and arms
and tells us he loves us.
Maybe it's in the blessing from the moon's soft kiss,
Or maybe it's somewhere in Buddha's belly,
Or perhaps in the fertile fruit of Mother Earth.
Maybe it's to be found in the colors of a painting,
Or in the contours of a sculpture.

We can indeed find so much.
We can uncover riches.
We can find ourselves loving others.
We can catch ourselves loving
every creature on the planet.
We may even look down at ourselves,
and catch a glimpse of ourselves
submerged in an array of love.
We can feel love from outside sources,
and even radiate love out.

However, when we don't love ourselves
something is missing.
We are incomplete as we go to bed,
Incomplete in our dreams,
Incomplete as we wake in the morning sun.
No one ever talks about it,
and mostly we are ashamed.
There must be something wrong with us we say.
Or maybe it just isn't meant to be.
We observe our surroundings and take count.
Assess whether or not it really exists.
When we don't love ourselves.
it's ever present, coloring our world.
We just can't shake it off.
We can't scrub it off
or peal it off.
We know this, because we try, and try, and try.
Everything is through our lens,
through our perspective.
Somehow, everything has to do with us,
and how it relates to our emptiness.
We become full with our emptiness,
and our search for meaning in life.
There is no room left for anything else.
We go this way and that,
but all in our own shoes.
We may even try to take off our shoes,

try on the shoes of another.
We let others try to tint our world,
But the thing is,
our world is tinted through us.
It is tinted with us.
We cannot remove ourselves.
We can never be anyone else,
It's unchangeable.

Oh yes, we can, and do find so much in
the corridors of life.
It's like museum full of relics.
We walk down the halls.
But when we gaze upon everything before us,
we interpret it all.
We are always interpreting.
We can find so much in all the places we search.
We can find little pieces of ourselves.
Collect what we might need
so that we can finally shine.

Funny, I do always wait for what I call
the "shine song" from my favorite artists, my favorite people.
I marvel at those who love themselves.
Not just those who say they do.
I especially marvel at those
who weren't born with it,
or lost it at an early age.
But then one day they find it, and we witness.
That's when we hear the special song with
a different tone, a different quality.
That's when we see that painting
that is different than all the ones before.
That is the day that the characters of the words on the page reflect
something entirely different.
It's the day the notes in the music are coming from a different place.
You can hear it.
You can see it.

You can feel it!
It's the most beautiful of the beautiful things to witness and notice!!

I want to say,
The search for self love is not in vain.
Because indeed we can find so many pieces of ourselves,
scattered across the universe, in all these places of which I speak.

The Treasure, Love is Found....

One day I was walking up the mountain,
Atalaya to be specific,
And there was no place left to look.
Not because I had exhausted all my options,
For the world is vast and options are limitless.
But rather, there was no place left to look
because I had found love for myself.
It was there, and it was real.
It was in all the particles gathered from my search.
I had finally found all the ingredients with which
to construct the perfect mirror of myself.
One that was accurate and not distorted.
And when I gazed upon myself,
When I saw my perfect reflection in this mirror
Which was finally re-constructed,
and carefully put together, it was there.
The image was perfect, the image was real.
And it brought tears to my eyes.
I saw my precious heart,
And it was mine, no others, it was mine.
The way that I love belonged to me.
The way that I cared and laughed and played,
It was me.
It was not a trick or slight of hand.
It wasn't something I was trying to make fit.
The compassion in the mirror belonged to me.
The blood pulsing through my veins was all mine.
I no longer studied an image trying to grasp an idea of me,
Instead, I witnessed myself.
I simply saw my own face.
I saw my immense kindness and it glowed.

I saw my unselfish heart.
I saw me breath forgiveness into the atmosphere.
I saw such a passionate, limitless being,
And then I saw my fragile-ness.
I saw all the parts within me that were so soft,
so smooth, so delicate.
This is where the most beautiful part of me resided.
This is where I could see someone that I loved.
I was not a jagged bar of steel,
But rather a flower in full bloom.
I was amazed, at how incredibly unique I was.
I was not a dime a dozen, like I had always believed myself to be.
I was irreplaceable.
I was most valuable in the raw.
I was someone I never wanted to lose ever again,
Someone I wanted to guard, cherish, protect.

For the first time, I was present in the atmosphere of my being.
For the first time I stopped thinking about me,
Instead I was me, and I could see who I was!

This Song is For Me

On another shore
where the lights meld into beautiful melodies
is my window into the most beautiful of all

I lie on my back
floating in the sea of eternity
lights dancing in my eyes

I'm bathed in fluid beauty
every moment suspended in the sky
levitating with delight

The sounds of our days echo through my flesh
rippling into my heart, drawn in by the warmth,
spreading through me head to toe
physically taking over me

My request to the heavens
…
Let this last till I depart,
let me bear witness to the smile
the effortless wonder of beauty

I'm enchanted and comforted
by the melodies covering me

Burry me in the sounds
of all that ever loved me in truth

The love received in honesty
is the love that sets me free
…………..
this song is for me!

Burning the candle at both ends!

Hey girl,
burning the candle at both ends
but of course mother dear,
it stops me from floating off
into the atmosphere

Roses don't smell nearly as sweet
in the garden of eternity,
the scent is divine
in the transience of time

When one gasp of breath
floods my senses
in the swaying abyss,
the rise and fall of ocean tides,
they cover me in what I need

Running at full speed,
under the stars
I'm shining there,
brighter than crystal snow,
reflecting back in this sea of black

I know how to elongate time,
stretch a minute to days
Momma, don't take it away
the faster I go
the slower it turns

I can transform
the scent of the earth

to a blanket of love,
the sound of a voice
to the song of my heart

Oh mother dear,
I don't fear the fall,
it brings me home
to what we are

The heat of the flame,
it closes in
to the center of me
I don't mind the fire,
not the dripping wax

The shifting shape of time,
that's my lullaby,
it's rocking comfort,
it's solace for my eyes

Sweet surrender deep
oh momma please,
don't take it away

Eastern Slopes

There is a taste, a feel
Kissing with the wind
Dancing in the cosmos
Being embraced by darkness
and light simultaneously
The sweetness of raindrops
on ones lips
Riding horse friend
on the Eastern slopes
faster than the wind
The vividness of the flowers
being interpreted from within
Opening ones wings
feeling the power of sky give flight
The sound of crisp white snow
and thin air in all its quietness
The beauty in stillness
with all it's power
Therein lies the memory of me
the essence of you

Dear Moon

Moon awakens my sense of sight
Painting the reality
of all that lies beneath his soft caress
Shadowed staircase
leading up to the heavens of dawn
Trees swaying in the dark
validate all that is my presence
I am cared for in the arms of the mountain
embraced by her sweet kindness
As birds softly come alive
with song in their heart
Each foothold on the earth
confirms my place to stand
Acknowledging the blood beneath my skin
Thank you dear moon
for illuminating my thoughts
for shining light upon my existence

Enough

You came into my life with one single word
to an endless string of expression
and you have been more than enough
I am content to call you friend
but even more, I am blessed
I am the grateful type
and you, the giving kind
It is enough to know you
and I am ecstatic that you subside
within my atmosphere
You are invited to stay as long as you wish
in whatever capacity you see fit
I ask for nothing from you, demand nothing
but I want it all, every last morsel I shall treasure
and if and when you should leave
you needn't ever say goodbye
I will only be happy that we crossed paths
and I will cherish the time that you gave me
as every minute has been clad in emeralds and yellow gold

Tia Madalena

I was beginning to write an ending where I drank my self away
Where a drink, even in secrecy was much better than what I felt
I leaned into this ending and it seemed possible, likely, even probable
Was most certainly doable, in my DNA for sure
And I thought of my mom's Tia Madalena who was an alcoholic
I recollect the story of how mom emptied all her liquor bottles
Slapped and pulled her out of bed by the hair
Told her to stop drinking or get out of their house
Mom was just eleven, and her Tia got her stuff and left for good
I wondered what Madalena's pain was like
The thought of her life was like a searing, gapping,
bleeding wound deep in my chest
Story was she was beautiful, funny, a genius
………..and a waste

I superimposed the image of Madalena with mine
and I saw myself flow out to sea with little substance
I was like the liquor mom poured out those years ago
I could see me, liquid and languid
with only enough strength to evaporate
………………
Erase, erase this all, erase this ending!
It isn't easy,
but this ending could be easy
It's safer than being me
And there are less people to hurt if I can stop being me
If I can stop feeling what I feel, there are less casualties, it's a fact
The consequences wouldn't be too bad, I am a happy drinker
More pleasant to be around, less tense, less afraid, likable even
Not so bad for the children

A subtly drunk mom is better than a crying mom
Better than an absent mom
Better than a mom who imagines bleeding to death
as she smiles and passes the salt
I can see it, I could get so lost in the liquor
not being able find my way out, even if I wanted to
I can tell how it would happen for me
The drink takes the edge off, helps you care a little less
The more you drink the less you care
Feeling less is like a vacation from yourself
Chronic drinking makes it more difficult to tolerate myself sober
It's easy to slide down this rabbit hole
and fade away right in front of everyone
without ever having to leave the room
..…....except for refills
Part of it is attractive, it's seductive
Especially if you can afford the good stuff
Especially if your body can tolerate it well
…………………..
NO, I don't want to live a life of disappearance!
Where I write myself out of my own narrative
perpetuating this indifference of self
And that's what I found myself pursuing
use alcohol to erase my feelings,
I actually started to erase myself, it's sweet amnesia
but it's amnesia, and amnesia has a point of no return

The interesting thing about this is that
you only erase yourself to you
The world still sees you
Mom still saw her Tia Madalena falling on the floor
People still see you slurring your speech, stumbling
Or maybe they see you laughing and being successful
But you see yourself less and less
You lose all your substance
Your pain becomes nondescript
which is the goal after all

....
But is this really what I want?
I want it somatically, viscerally
But cognitively, NO
I think I'm supposed to live....
I can't go out like this!

Tossing and Turning

Restless tonight
missing friends that knew me well
Laughing, loving and playing into the night
I see the smoke swirling around me
in the dim light of the in between
It touches my bareness and enters
all the crevices that lay awake
contemplating the night
I inhale and am slightly intoxicated
by its existence
It engulfs me with a kind of
knowingness I crave
I accept it and invite it in
quite uninhibited
I want to take it in to my depths
I feel it cover me and explore my existence
with the curiosity of water wanting to flow
It lingers on my neck
whispers thoughts in my ears,
I tingle, wanting it to slowly
work it's way inside me
through my thoughts,
my beating heart,
my every pore,
I hear the dialogue tell me no,
Find a way to stop!
Yet the smoke beckons me
and I suffer alone in my addictions
This is what it's like

to lay in isolation,
With my partner awake beside me,
Restless in his own sea,
Unbeknownst to me

Starving Santa Fe Bears

I hear drifting in
with the moonlit sky
the rumbling of starvation.
The mistaken rumor of selflessness
is carried on the blackened wings
of high achievers
in hopes of wearing white,
dreaming of some deity
which was only written in part.
Do not starve yourself,
less you become ravenous.
Do not deny yourself pleasure,
it is the food of life.
Once starving
you cannot overcome the urge to eat.
Self-control will flee,
all left is a voracious creature
consuming with reckless abandon
doing what it takes to survive.

Cristo Rey

Bless Me Father for I have sinned………..
I can't help but silently recite the Act of Contrition
as my feet enter the church
I smell the incense and my eyes fall
upon the beautiful alter
I look up at the Vigas and carvings
and the morning sunshine filters in
through the trees and windows
dappling the saints with color
I kneel in prayer beside my
children and husband
I am taken back to various points in my life
Where I sought the comfort of church
just to make it through the day
Memories that are tucked safely within
come back

I remember searching for an unlocked,
empty church in Las Vegas
Looking for a place to lay my head
let my body slump into its telling form
A place where I needn't be upright
A place where tears could flow
On many occasions I landed in the parking lot of
Saint Joseph Husband of Mary
For I was hurting too much to drive responsibly
and had no place to break down and feel safe
Somehow this strikes me as superbly funny
Given the state I was in, barely hanging on, wishing I was dead

Well, I liked Saint Joseph, he was a carpenter, a loving father,
he was always there
This was my church, very large, empty, quiet, dark in the middle of day
Just a few small stained glass windows let enough
light in to stop me from tripping
I slipped in through the side door
so I wouldn't have to answer any questions
I maneuvered myself to the far corner where it was darkest
I would find a pew where I wouldn't be seen and I would lay flat
Placing my head upon the smooth wooden surface
And with a deep breath of relief, my eyes would burn and fill with tears
Eventually my body would curl into the fetal position
and I would cover myself with my sweater
The church bench was cold and hard
with the air conditioner running on high
Pushing cold air onto my body
Giving me goosebumps
On occasion,
if I heard people enter the church
I would slip onto the floor
Hiding behind the kneelers
I would hold my tears and sobs until
the church was empty once again
I couldn't handle seeing another human
There was no one friendly or accepting
enough for all the things I carried
Perhaps only Jesus
I would notice my puddle of tears on the floor
and somehow it felt appropriate
and insane all at once
In those moments
I was pretty sure no one had ever felt as I did
Lying there in a deserted church, on the dirty floor,
an educated adult, with a house, a car, friends, family,
sobbing like a little child
Wanting strength, answers
and to simply feel ok

I usually only had a couple of hours
before I had to be someplace
Or before the church would get busy, or locked up
I would lie there for as long as I could
Just wanting to disappear from the world, needing a break
Feeling so alone, desperate for comfort

Many times in my life I sought
Solace in church, it seemed safer than
Seeking it from a person
And I hoped to encounter Jesus
A being I could trust with my suffering,
my heartache, pain, well being, and my survival
No living, breathing human
knew how to hold me

It's amazing that I walk into this church
600 miles away from the one in the hot desert
And the years have passed, and I find it remarkable
that I'm standing

God's Embrace

Love deeply without fear.
Mourn, cry and feel pain,
but please let the beauty in life sustain you.
That flower when pain is in your heart,
the vague scent of peach as you walk by,
the sunset or sunrise painting the sky on your darkest days,
that is your God embracing you, he loves us so much!!!

Unqualified (a passage of personal importance)

It was in a rose garden maze, I found my place upon a bench. The tears had finally gone dry and there was no air left in my lungs. I literally was gasping, afraid, not knowing where there was to go from here. I just couldn't handle anymore, my heart physically ached I had such a strong pain in my chest, my limbs were so heavy and felt dead, as if the blood had already left them and was about to stop pulsing through my body. Willing my body to move took more effort than I had in me.

I sat on the bench for hours, from the morning light to the now evening sky. I cried and cried in agony, like it could release some of my horror. I couldn't move, I no longer knew how. There wasn't enough space in the air to hold my pain and provide oxygen at the same time, it just didn't seem possible. And at this point, I knew it was actually possible to die of a broken heart.

My heart was shattered. Just a day before, the nurse handed me my daughter's lifeless body, no bigger than a pear. She asked if I wanted to hold her. I was so afraid, but I said yes, thinking it would give me closure, wanting the realness to matter in some way that would help me understand what had occurred. I had read that if a mother didn't see, touch, hold, her baby she could lose touch with reality. Now all I wanted to do was lose touch with my sickening reality. Pretend it wasn't real. Pretend that my dead fetus, my daughter didn't look perfect to me.

She was supposed to be deformed. The descriptions I had read described the abnormal proportions, the grotesque figure that was growing within me. DNA testing, modern technology, imaging showing a heart full of holes. Carrying her to term was going to endanger my life, and certainly leave me unable to conceive more

74

children. I didn't want to leave my perfect 1 year old without a mother, I wanted to give her a sibling for life, not one that would die shortly after birth. All I could do is see my toddlers face when I signed the paperwork allowing the poison to kill my fetus and not me.

I tried to fool myself into thinking that the logic behind my choice was enough. I ran all the numbers, the cost of all the surgeries to try and keep my unborn daughter alive, all my days in the hospital if I was to make it through. All this money we didn't have, decreasing the quality of life of my husband and daughter, of me. I studied the graphs, charted the suffering of what would be endured if I was to keep her. The years spent in hospitals, only to bury her. She wouldn't have a life outside hospitals and probably not make it more than a couple of years, if at all. What would this do to my family? I quantified it all, as to point me in the right direction.

Neither, priest, nor surgeons, nor doctors, nor husband could make this choice for me. I prayed, I prayed and I prayed, and I was completely alone. This was my burden, no one was willing to take it from me. No one wanted this blood on their hands, and no one was willing to tell me I should keep her, not one of my advisors. So many statistics, I let science choose for me. Risk versus benefits, with or without her, for the projected future of everyone I loved. An educated guess based on research. Pros and cons, maintain order, maintain an ounce of control, predict the future. What would it be, sacrifice her 1% chance of life for the possibility of a bright future for the the rest of us? Could I watch my flesh and blood suffer in pain as we tried to make her live, knowing she would die, was this even humane to any of us, much less her? Could I handle her blood on my hands? The statistics said I could and my decision was justifiable, the responsibility was all mine.

However, when they handed her lifeless body to me I didn't know how beautiful she would be. I forgot that I was a mother. I forgot that I would love her more than I loved myself. I forgot that all I would see was her beauty, her imperfectly perfect form. I forgot that for a mother to kill her child is unnatural under any circumstance, logical or not. I knew I was risking my soul in this choice, but I didn't know my soul might be worth something someday. I knew that someday I would have to face God, but I never knew that someday I would find God inside me. I didn't know what this would be like. Carrying the knowledge of my decisions, irrevocable, with God in my heart, remembering it all. Knowing that the best I had was an educated guess, but a guess nonetheless, this was such a cruel reality.

I wanted it to end, I wanted me to end, I wanted my suffering to end, I didn't know how I could ever go home and be a good mom when I was capable of sacrificing my own child. I could not breath, I could not breath, I could feel myself dying. I didn't want to live, but I couldn't stand to die and leave my daughter without a mom, I felt so helpless. All the warmth had left my body, my flesh was was growing cold. Blood was no longer circulating as it once had. It was ice in the desert, freezing me over, turning my fingers blue. Freezing my thoughts to standstill, to quietness, emptiness, blankness. I was becoming blank, I was getting erased, and I drew in more air, trying to find my will to live.

Then I smelled it. It was like peaches and nectarines scenting the air and it helped me inhale once more. How could anything smell so beautiful, HOW?? I focused my eyes which had been staring off into nothingness and never had I ever seen such a thing of beauty. It was a single yellow orange rose before me. It was so incredibly vivid, the color was so rich, swirling softly onto itself. It was so saturated in color in a colorless world. I reached to stroke it's soft petals, and it sent warmth back into me through my fingertips, so soft and silky, like running your finger across the hand of God. When I swallowed I could taste the sweetness in the air, sending so many messages of goodness to my brain. Such stillness in the world existed at this moment, and I noticed the sound of a soft breeze rolling between it all, sushing my despair. The breeze rose and fell like a song of love, touching my skin, stroking my hair, making the leaves dance and embracing me with such love. How did I notice this, how was I even capable? I couldn't believe how amazing God could be to give me such incredible beauty, it was enough to sustain life!!! I allowed the beauty to envelope me and I noticed how incredibly much God loved me. This singular rose, it allowed me to breath once again. I was blown away at how beautiful life could be during such a time of darkness. The contrast was stark and it was unforgettable to feel God loving me at such a time. I was humbled, feeling so unworthy and loved at the same time, all I could say was thank you.

I don't know if I did the right thing. To think I know is somewhat delusional and there is a very good chance I did the wrong thing. I will not have the luxury of knowing in this lifetime. This is my reality. I do know that I loved this life that grew within me, not like an acquaintance but like a mother, this is the most painful thing. I also know that God loves me like a daughter, not like an acquaintance, and this is beauty beyond belief.

The Best Day

I am mom, my arms are soft, they are strong, and they are steady
They will hold you and cradle you in the coldest storm
My bosom is your sanctuary, it is the closest place to my heart
And for you it will never grow cold
This is my promise, it comes from my soul, it transcends this life of mine
My heart is the place where you were first conceived
It is the place where you will always have belongings
My heart knew you before you ever took your first breath
And my heart shall know you with no bodily form
I have never wanted anything more than to have you join me
To have you know me, and mostly for me to know
The sound of your footsteps walking the earth
I will do my best to convert my humble gatherings
Of both matter and knowledge
To the provisions from which you can grow
Your destiny does not belong to me,
It is yours and the heavens to negotiate upon
But I, I will provide you a platform from which to launch your dreams
And a place to safely land all your creations
You will find your home in the world,
My home however, will always be yours
You are only tethered to me if you wish, you though are in fact my home
My anchors are cast into your waters
Take from me the parts which will help you love
My eyes, my heart, my humor, the things that breath life
When you look upon a mirror
The best parts of me are yours to grow from within
I will work and do my best to create memories
So that on days when sentimentality pays you a visit
It will be in your ultimate favor
You shine and I shall rejoice, let this give you lift

My love is here to bolster your path
And cushion the things that are difficult
I am unyielding
I am mom

Crippled Children

I am handicapped
From the inside
I learned this when I was eight
I was crippled
Underneath my skin
It was hard to figure out
But it was a fact
Because my medical record
Fit in a stack
Filed in alphabetical order
At the big hospital
With all the broken children
I was different
I wasn't normal
And it hurt at first
Because it would have been nice to fit in
But very soon I figured out
The mold wasn't meant for me
And very soon I was glad
The mold wasn't meant for me
Instead my eyes were opened
To an entire different universe
Hidden underneath my skin
Very soon I learned
How to see someone's heart
Whether they were a ten
Or only had fifty percent of their limbs
And very soon I learned
iQ was just a chart
Intelligence came in many flavors
And truth was often difficult to decipher

Because math didn't always add up
And sometimes, one plus one made three
And sometimes mirrors lied
Because they didn't always reveal
When someone's spine was twisted
When blood was missing a component
Or when someone was immaculate
Beneath torn and filthy clothing
And soon I learned
Mirrors are for identification only
Because even the most distorted
Because even the most wealthy
And even the most beautiful of all
Are so much more
Then those things
Visible on the surface
And yes,
I may not fit the mold
And somethings might be broken
However, I am actually not handicapped
And crippled is just a word

True Fable

I learned about unconditional love one day after the rain
A beautiful, spotted little toad emerged from the mud and I loved him
He was like a gift of love from heaven
He was the brightness in my blackened day
It was one of those days that you pray for just one little
ounce of happiness because the clouds decided to rain on
you for a little too long, and you don't think you can take much more
This perfect, beautiful little toad came climbing out from the mud
which had been nothing but parched dirt in the weeks prior
This little toad was a miracle and the answer to my prayers
He was my PROOF that there was a God,
and I was so ecstatic that he arrived!
He was like the prince who emerged from the fairytale
to save me from the darkness
I loved this little creature so and wanted to keep him forever!
So I gently held him, and I placed him
in the ample pocket of my coveralls
which I had lined with dirt, and I snapped the pocket shut
I thought he could work with me until I had a break
and could make him a better place to live
I planned to take him home
When I went to check on my swell little prince, he wasn't the same
One of his little legs was broken, he could no longer hop
He was so delicate even though he had emerged from the dirt after
the longest slumber in the drought
Such a miraculous creature, such a delicate creature
My heart shattered for wanting to hold on to
something that I loved so much
It should have been enough to see him, but it wasn't, I wanted more
I desperately wanted more of the love that was gifted to me by the rain
Naively, I wanted him for my very own

From that moment I understood how to love and how to not love
You simply cannot take more than you are given

The most beautiful flowers remain the ones you never pick

Dark Side of The Moon

It is all the noise and disorderly emotions
when emerging from a field of flowers
that proclaims the glory of this world
...
It is the contrast that pushes us to evolve
it is the beauty when knowing the pain
which can propel us to change
in ways which are profound
....

Cacophony of a Broken Neck

When I look in the mirror I look similar to the day before
…..my neck is broken, but my eyes aren't bleeding
I can still move my legs and my face looks the same…….
But when I move my neck,
it's loud and screaming inside my head………
………yet, my hair still shines and curls as the day before

No one can hear the screaming, high pitched
disorderly screeches that accompany my breathing
……..No supernatural sounds emanate from my body
and when I stand, moth wings flutter in my ears
 ……..they often cause me to vomit
However, only the monarch outside my window can be observed

My skin feels like its burning with boiling water poured upon me
……….yet it isn't even red……….
…………..there are no fluid filled vesicles,
rather it is golden and beautiful from the summer's sun
………This is what is seen as my husband strokes my skin

I can barely lift or hold my head straight………
…it feels as if it weighs one hundred pounds
but if you saw me you wouldn't understand why,

My proportions appear normal
………I appear to be whole
…………..I appear to possess great health
You cannot smell the acids and sugars
blending into a maddening mixture of chaos
when I swallow my own spit…….
….you cannot taste the brokenness that I do

None of this is visible in my reflection
............not even to me
I study it and I am baffled
.............I am amazed that I cannot see any of it
The reality outside my body
.........doesn't match the intense pain which lies within
I am unable to consolidate reality...........

If a picture is worth a thousand words
It is also worth a million more untold

Decorator Crab

The cold ocean breeze makes my face tingle
Little droplets of water saturate me with the sea
Cloaked with a new identity by the ocean mist
I am no longer a desert lizard or raven up in the sky
or even the human with a family, career, a house
Today I am the little decorator crab scuttling in the tide pools
and we are one as creatures living
I admire and marvel at the way he wears
his prized possessions upon his head
He adorns himself with the ones he loves most
the ones which comfort and provide such safety
He covers himself in colors and textures of splendor
all the things which bring him most joy
He hasn't any shame whatsoever
to take what he fancies most
and make his own
He doesn't care to be original
but in his quest of beautiful disguises
he is indeed one of a kind...........
.........My legs are curled on the cold sand
with the tide coming in,
Waves crash upon the shore
inching closer and closer to my heart
I sense the ocean knows me
she wishes to make me fluid once again
The water calls me despite her cold standoffish front
The wind tangles my land dwelling hair
obscuring my face to the world
I rub soft pebbles of sand between my fingers
shedding my coat upon a smooth beached log
I end my internal battle with the cold

knowing all I need to do is breath
I can now see the fire inside me
is enough to keep me warm
My shoes and socks are left behind
I peel layers of clothing away
my bare skin now bathed by the sun
I brush the sand upon my body till I glisten and glitter
I'm like the children who haven't yet forgotten how to play……..
…………..…..I cover myself with thoughts of those I love
Red-Orange starfish placed upon my lap
Stories once shared atop my head
Carefully crafting my mother of pearl and seaweed crown
I adorn myself with all my favorite parts of others
letting the air they have once exhaled
come find me in the wind
I wrap my heart in everything
that has ever made me swell with love
and I haven't any shame whatsoever
I simply feel comfort and safety
allowing the beauty of my favorites
to decorate me in colors and textures divine
and with each and every jewel
I am as beautiful as the ocean

Four AM March

I stepped into the moonlit shadows beyond my doorway
The cool damp earth beneath my feet, smell of
rain and trees, infusing the morning night
The silver and black contrast of earth to sky, so overwhelmingly beautiful
I welcome you into my awareness and dedicate this quadrant of time
to you my dear friend

I breath in the air and feel alive
For you I take count

When the earth starts to shake beneath our feet,
is when nature inevitably reaches out her hands to caress and hold us
The details of all that is good and right become magnified in the
midst of uncertainty
Grateful to drink in the lush air and feel my legs move swiftly
beneath me
Rhythmic breathing cleanses the body of all that is fowl,
leaving behind the promise of perfection in a moment,
elongated by the senses

Sight, smell, texture, sound, taste,
every little morsel of time under a microscope
is wrapped up like a birthday present for you, complete with a bow

How lucky we are to step into our minds,
with thoughts of our elected ones, and simple sweet laughter.
Images of bright sparkly jewels reflected in someone's eyes
are there for the taking

These nuggets of mind play,
simultaneous with the present experience of time, so brilliantly flavored

I do love the perfect darkness when soaked in the starry sky

At this moment, I wish you all the love on earth,
in whichever form you fancy

Such a perfect gift of love I have for you and all you hold dear,
for you and your loved ones

When I step out into the beauty of nighttime
my silence turns to an anthem of love for you my dear friend

Ode to Papa

He is the weaver
of a tapestry of earth and sky
He brings threads together
where green and blue
run alongside one another
barely touching
then side by side
One thread above
and one below
sometimes completely separate
He approximates their distance
to meet in the space between
One goes over
One goes under
one to the right
and one to the left
one in the light
the other in the shadow
The patterns are in his head
where both yarns are needed
to make the fabric of life
that can hold
the gleaming future
in sacredness
He becomes the needle
we become the thread
One must pass through his eye
to see the course
of the path he leads
He sees what others miss
He pulls and pushes

in the ways that plead
To be led in his direction
is actually a journey
through his heart
For his heart
is the needle
and we have passed
through his heart
like many before
and many will after
Some may never notice,
How could I not?

Consumer of Musical Ecstasy(For Led Zeppelin and the Posies-Thank You, Flood of Sunshine)

Cosmic conversation from above
I hear you echo out to me
Across the land from another shore
Through the slippage of time
Your love becomes suspended
Souls lift to the sky
My view from the stands is clear
Immortal you become
As your love professed
In every language
For all to hear
Painted with sounds divine
I hear the Sistine Chapel
Your love rises from the sea
You pull me across time
Into the arms of two lovers
Celestial and infinitely beautiful
Your conversation stitches
One dimension to another
Pure inspiration from above
You push and pull, rise and fall
I hear your voices
They are overlaid and separate
They alternate, and dance
Fast, slow, skipping a beat
Till all instruments become one
And I am lifted to the heavens
How beautiful it is
The creation of love

From one song to another
Illuminating the path
To a state of pure nirvana

May Showers

Monsoons, when are you going to return?
I have grown accustomed to your arrival in the Spring
Beginning with a sprinkling here and there
teasing me with the idea of you
making my imagination soar in great anticipation
Images of floral crowns and succulent berries abound
I can see myself dancing in the rain
drinking your sweet elixir
after your clouds gather into one giant sea of moisture
bursting open above my head
above the garden I have sowed

Monsoons, you have been so faithful to me,
but there isn't a cloud in the sky
It feels so empty without a trace of you
All I see is a vast space of blue
which has begun to turn to grey
and now ash falls instead of your sweet drops

Be not mistaken
there is such a void in my heart
where it once was so full
and I must admit, I am a bit confused

Did I expect too much from you?
Was I beginning to lean on the joy your showers bring
wanting to make everything sparkly and clean,
wanting everything to glisten,
including me?
Did I revel in too many long showers,
soaking up your sweet gifts,

splashing my own face
thinking of the next time I would feel your drops
as if it was written in stone
as if you were mine to own?

Did I finally contaminate your pristine beauty
with all the debris you help me clean?
Are you now struggling to rid yourself of all the pollutants
diverting your waters to your true Northern Skies
so that they can run pure once again?

Oh, I know you don't belong to me Sweet Rain
you are a gift for all
and you have so much work to do
from the four directions of the wind
everyone has gardens to grow
I know I'm not the only one
I know its difficult to be everywhere at once
And it must be exhausting
the demands of our sometimes reckless race
I pray we didn't make you ill
depleting you of all the elements you need to thrive
I fear I took to much, perhaps more than my share
I'm so sorry sweet rain, I'll try and do better

I do know I have grown so attached
It's just that you are so beautiful
It's the way you make everything shine
even in the faintest light
It's the way you saturate colors back to life
Everything in your presence is more vivid
more beautiful, more meaningful
and it's so impossibly difficult
to not want more of you

Dear Monsoons, do you know
that the fires now burn?
They run wild without your dampening

The flames grow ever higher
all the tangled heaps are being turned to ash,
and both prized possessions and careless waste
are being diminished to dust
With the threat of the flames
we are forced to see what matters most
we are forced to see one another amongst these tumultuous winds

Oh Sweet Rains, have you left us alone intentionally so we can
burn?
Are you allowing our attachments to turn to smoke?
Is this your way of giving us wings?
Letting us extinguish our own embers,
letting the flames burn
through all thats dead and down

Oh dear Monsoons
I wish you only knew
I'm sorry for holding too tight
I'm sorry for taking more than my share
and I'm sorry for requiring so much watering
I know I need to be strong in your absence
I know you are a privilege
not an entitlement

You have probably heard this before
after you have filled so many reservoirs with water
you eventually evaporate
and empty buckets remain
only to echo in loneliness once again,
waiting for your luscious drops

And I think you might be aware
I have yet to learn the art of gathering clouds
and bursting them back to fluid drops of water
And I think you know
all this sublimation will never amount to Rain

So please, just know that I know this
and know that I am working on it in earnest
And I struggle to pray for your arrival
as much as I struggle to not pray for it
But mostly, I pray that your OK
I also do know,
beautiful Monsoons,
You were never mine to begin with

Mighty Beautiful Elephants

I admire the Elephants
They are so powerful
They mourn their dead
better than most humans
as if they know something we do not
They understand their own uniqueness
They know not one single creature
can be replaced
This is why they have such long life spans
It is their beauty, they value life
They possess such empathy
They feel all the emotions
Fear, Anger, Sadness, Joy, and Love
They are closely acquainted with God
They know they only have
so much time on this earth
to love and to feel
and they are so brave
They cry in broad daylight
for all to see
I bow to the elephants

Guitar Man's Promise (Bread)

Enter into the burning fires of passion
Fly high and dive into the deepest waters
You will not drown, I promise you
You will not fall out of the sky
I know the way to solid ground

Fall deeply in love, give it all you have
Taste it, devour it, completely saturate yourself in love
Wrap yourself in every morsel of emotion
Allow the chemicals to rush through your system
It is safe, you will not lose your form, I promise you
You will not disintegrate and you will not explode
I will keep you complete
I will guide you back home

Enter into the realm of fear
Let your heart race, your hands grow ice cold
Let the fear paralyze you,
Let it make you run as fast as you can,
Let it make you fight
You do not have to avoid this space,
You will survive, I will protect you
You will come out whole, more intact than ever before
Just follow me

Cry, submerge yourself in sadness, feel every bit of it
Feel it under your skin, let it engulf your thoughts
Let it render your legs useless
Allow it to suck the air out of your lungs
Allow it to disrupt your digestive system
Go all the way down to the very bottom

I will pull you back up, I know how
The secret is now yours
I promise, you will once again rejoice

Let anger burn down the house
Tear apart the walls,
Shred them all to pieces
Let it show no mercy
Allow your eyes to see red
I promise you, your fire will burn out
And new growth will come again
In even greater beauty
I will show you what comes next

Feel joy and happiness to the greatest extent
Laugh till your stomach aches,
Tingle with anticipation
Let flowers sprout from every crevice
And the waters to sparkle like diamonds
Enjoy the beauty, taste it, feel it , memorize it
IT will not be the last time,
I promise you

Follow me, I know the way......

(For the Victims of Charles Manson, My Dearest Friend Natalie Vasquez and the endless list of innocent victims of terror)

Victims

My Heart is broken for all those touched by evil

Sometimes the rug is pulled out from under our feet
and we spiral to the edge of life
with so much despair and fear
We are terrified beyond belief
and it is rightfully so
as we have been touched by something crippling
and horrific beyond belief
The kind of evil that is unmistakable
the kind that brutally massacres
severs heads, stabs and destroys with the deepest brutality
It has no regard for any life
it steals so much from us
it rocks our beliefs to the core
leaves us questioning God
Such intention of evil
is so impossible to understand
and many of us leave at this point
We can no longer bear to stay
Some of us get taken against our will
kicking and screaming
Still, many of us remain
and we barricade our hearts or ourselves
in defense of ever being touched by evil again
Yet it remains, and we can only look away
But it's residue attaches to us
Changing us forevermore

Many say there is no understanding evil
but what of those who've tried
Those who have gone to meet evil in its realm
What if we sat across the table from it
and spoke directly to it
What if we attempted to understand it from the inside
What if we could stop shaking and let go of our fears
Could we stomach its origins?
Could we survive?
What would it take?
......Bravery of the highest order
......Willingness to hear the answers
......Sacrifice of epic proportions
......Faith in the goodness that lies within
......And faith in the goodness that lies without

This is for all those who have dueled with evil
and come out victorious, those who did not crumble
those who did not succumb, those who live amongst us
and joyfully proclaim the beauty of this wonderful life!!!
………………..…………………………………..
…………………I AM ME……………..………
………………………………………………………..

I Am Me

I am Me
I am wanted
I am loved and I am cherished
My heart expands from birth
and I grow as the tree of knowledge and life
I am fed by science, nature and God
and by the people who surround me
They bless me as I sleep, they love me as I play
I drink from the glass of festivity and truth
and I know the pleasure of this bountiful earth
It comes to me as honey from the bee
as tubers from the earth
I connect my dots in the sky
and read my constellations
knowing how lucky I am to breath
how wonderful it is to have wings
Then one day, in the sweetest air of summer fun
evil brushed up against my skin
And it was so vile, so putrid that I could not scrub it off
I lay paralyzed inside my nest till it became a darkened cave
And the earth began to crumble beneath my weakening flesh
My wings were singed and soaking wet, I could no longer fly
and the days turned to weeks, to months and on and on
I knew what it is that had to be done
There was only one way out for me
It was right through the eye of the storm
inside of me and in the fields of war beyond my door
I knew I must enter into the lair of all that threatened my existence
I must lie my weakened body next to the savage animals
which were already consuming me alive
I had to consume evil and drink from the same glass

This meant to gain physical proximity to my fears
it meant to enter evil's mind, to befriend it
to live with it, breath it, smell it and feel it enter my soul,
and so I did…………….
I basked in evil and smothered myself
in all that was revolting to my heart
I did it carefully and methodically with complete control
I found my strength beneath my wings
and I saw that my lungs could once again breath
I gained access to the mind and heart of the most frightening of all
the one most capable of slaughtering humans
without ever lifting a finger
The one grown of anger and hatred
inside the belly of institutions
stripped of love and compassion
but with high intellect set on destruction
The thoughts of the most vile
entered my mind through doors swung open
The instincts of the most hateful
were felt inside my flesh as if we were one
My eyes became as his and so did my ears
and my body was one with all that was covered in death

I became so close and intimate with all my fears
and with he who was so revolting
I was deep inside, dancing with evil
side by side, between two worlds
and when I caught sight of my reflection
I saw something so remarkable
I shall never, ever, EVER forget
I could see ME!
ME, I remained intact!
In fact, I was more intact than ever before
And with such clarity I saw myself as complete
and I noticed that when I relinquished my fear
That my eyes were mine, my ears were mine,
but most importantly, my intellect, my heart
and my soul were all mine

I belonged to ME and I knew what ME meant
I saw the line that separates us one from another
And I saw clearly,
the darkness
that had entered my bed,
it was not ME!
And the vile, putrid, evil, hateful thoughts
that I had accessed
they were NOT mine!!
And this was the blessing of all blessings
to simply be ME
and to be alive!!
My individuality was my greatest strength,
my greatest gift to be cherished
Right then and there, in my reflection
I saw so clearly
that fear itself was
the only passageway for evil
and that I had nothing to fear!

My Heart Needs a Bandaid

God please help me
This is a new kind of prayer
because the old kind isn't serving anyone anymore
Today I will not ask for what I have asked for
every day since I first started talking to you
Today I will not ask you to fix me or improve upon me
Today I will not ask for the rest of the world to feel loved
Today I will kick everyone out of the room
I don't want anyone in here but me
I ask You, I beg You, Please….
Help me see myself alone in the room
Let it be devoid of all the fallen bodies ever-present
Get them all out, so I can see myself
So someone can see me

God please, don't keep me alive for my children
Don't keep me alive for my mom
Don't keep me alive for those who would mourn my departure
You know this is the reason I have stayed
You know this!
I don't want to stay for anyone else today
Today I'm not asking to make me a better person
So I can hurt others less
I'm not asking for you to help me benefit the world,
rather than harm it
Don't help me make up for the way I have hurt others
Today I need to take the day off
no amends, none
Don't take away my disfunction
that's not what I am asking for
Don't change me, don't clean me up

don't help me see the light
Don't make me wiser, or kinder, or better
I can't today, I can't even lift my legs
not today, I want to sit alone
completely alone and ask You to help me for Me

God please
Help me heal my broken heart
And I say to You
My heart aches
Not someone else's heart
Mine
I feel deep pain
I am wounded
I am exhausted
I am beat up
I am in need of love
Forgiveness
Kindness
Understanding
Please help me feel comforted
Give me warmth
Give me peace
But please
Please, give me love
The kind that I need
Please patch me up
Bandaids only
No massive reconstruction
Palliative care alone
Wipe away my tears
Hold me in your heart
Hold me in your prayers
Hold me as a child in the most need
Your child
Just for today
This I ask
Help me walk

Give me nourishment
Feed me as your helpless child
because I can't lift the spoon to my mouth
Stick an IV in my arm
I can't swallow anymore
I have swallowed enough
Take me out from under the heavy weight
of my failures and shortcomings
I need a break from my past
Let me lie weightless in the warm oceans
till I am better, stronger
Give me the love I need
I, Me, Myself am hurt, and I'm bleeding
Please place bandaids on my gashes, my cuts
I don't care if I deserve it
My blood is red like everyone else's
and I can't get up
Give me compassion for being hurt
regardless of why
Let it only matter that I was hurt
and that I need love
Don't ask me what I did to cause this
just help me, take away my sobs
I just want love
No questions asked
Let me be loved for me
with all my unsightly imperfections
Naked and bleeding
Love me anyhow
Just for the day
No fixing
Love me anyhow

Issac

Why do you put the needle in your arm?
Why do you want to die?
Do you really think a needle from your Dentist
Is more frightening than the one from the streets?

Oh Issac, I know that you do.
But why?
Have you failed to find meaning?
Was life too cruel?
Or was it happenstance?
A hit here and there and before you knew it
You had succumbed?

What happened, do you remember how beautiful you were?
Was this intentional?
Was life too painful?
Were you just having fun?

I'm so sorry for your pain.
I can see it in your eyes.
You don't have to be ashamed.
I can see you.
I know life can be brutal.
Don't shrink from me.
Don't hide.
I can see you,
And your beautiful,
Track marks and all.
I wish you could believe it.

It's so painful I know
This little part of you that hasn't given up.
This is the part that hurts the most,
Because there still exists
The shadow of what could have been,
Or the the thought of what could still be.

It's not over yet.
I wish I could help you.
I only have love for you.
So much love and I'm not sure where it goes,
Or if you can feel it.
I am so sorry.
Isaac, it's not over.

Reach For the Pear

The boy sees what is right in front of him
It is within his reach
But he doesn't dare want it
He stops himself cold

Everything is new,
everything is pristine, foreign
and so capable of being destroyed

However………..
without wanting
he will never reach out
to take hold of that which is right in front of him

The child will never reach for that which he does not know how to
want

This is important to know…...

And so there is something to be truly sad
about……………………………..
………………………………..

Someone, make him reach for the fucking pear dangling on the tree!!
Because I will bet you, if he doesn't reach, that pear is gonna fall on
the ground and rot……

Make the child reach!

Make him fucking reach!!!!!!!!
He needs help.
He doesn't know how to want it.

Notes from a Random Day in May
Being Content vs. Being Ambitious

Can ambition and contentment live in the same room?
Yes. Only with open doors.
Do not confuse "wanting" with ambitions.
It is OK to have ambitions?
Yes, it is in fact imperative that you do.
It is OK to want something and have a goal?
It is OK to want to obtain that which you do not have.
The caveat being, that it must be a very well calculated goal
which is driven by thought and not emotion.
No upside down volcanoes allowed.
There must be boundaries surrounding ones ambitions
or things will easily interfere and cause them to go haywire,
therefore preventing one from attaining.
Ambitions MUST be rational.
If not rational, big red flag.
Also, never, never, NEVER let your penis decide what you want,
you will never be content, this is where one becomes insatiable.
The more aligned with being rational and honorable your goal, the better.
This will lead to greater happiness and greater contentment.

Humble Student,
Miss No longer believing the Fallacies

Dear Unknown Soldier of Love

I felt your love today
I might be crazy
But I felt it come to me through the atmosphere
Warm particulate filled sparkly air
Brimming with sweet fragrances of the summer's harvest
It tasted like the end of a season and the beginning of a new one
It rushed in from the dome of our planet
Somewhere under the ozone
In bright rays of sunshine
It entered my space from all sides, all encompassing
It was in beautiful melodic waves
You came to me and sang, I love you, gently in my ear
And right into my core
You squeezed me tightly with joy
And you didn't want to let go of me
You held me in the highest regard
With an admiration and respect I had never felt before
I gave you joy and filled you up
And you desired madly to fill me with all things good
To the degree you became overwhelmed
And then your heart turned over
Like a leaf in the breeze
Revealing itself in a colorful array
To a full expression of love
I felt the flutter in your heart
I closed my eyes basking in this amazingness
I froze time as to never forget
And this love enveloped me fully in a way I had never felt before
Perhaps it was all my imagination, maybe it was my deepest desire
But I felt it clearly

And I have no idea what it means
Other than I now know how it feels
To be loved by this unknown soldier of love

Just a Woman

Now it doesn't really matter, does it?

All these things we feel in the recesses of our hearts,
Of our minds.
For the most part,
There is extreme passion
Which lives underneath our pulsing bodies
Underneath our heaving breath
And it all gets dispersed as energy to the atmosphere
In our cries, in our moans, in our silent prayers
Attempting to be good people
Attempting to lock it in
However, we just can't help ourselves from having desires
From wanting
From needing
From being thirsty
As children,
Imagining water in the Sahara
I'm curious
How many of us were designed like this?
Am I a singular man?
Am I an honest man?
Perhaps I'm just a woman.
…….Filled with love.
…………Filled with fire.
………………..Filled with passion.
…………………….……Filled with desire.

PS:

Why Didn't anyone tell me it was OK to love people deeply?
Why Didn't they tell me I could love Men and Women alike?
Why didn't they tell me alI I needed was boundaries?
Instead I followed fear
Thinking it wold keep me safe
I clipped my own wings
Boxed up my own heart for one alone
Tapped it shut and forgot to even leave breathing holes
It was suicide from the get go
It isn't meant to be this way
We are made to Love
I was made to Love

PPS:

I skipped school the day they covered boundaries
I think I was out sick
My belly ached and I needed to figure out how people got pregnant
I stayed home rewriting all the rules
There was a giant gust of wind and all my labels went flying everywhere
And I couldn't remember which rules belonged under which columns
I tried to categorize things correctly
Love and Sex got placed in the same box
I sealed them up tight
Trying to keep myself safe
Not to bad for an 9 year old
Working alone, under the roof of a safe home
Boy do I wish I had made it to school that day
They didn't cover boundaries again till 4 decades later
This time I sat in the front row

Gas Station Coffee

High on the Brazilian Stone
Perched curiously out of place
Sat a styrofoam cup
From my household inhabitants it was not
From my own hands it did not come
From days gone by
It was clearly mine
Transported from the past
Reminder of days transformed
I step through the portal
Instantly taken aback by the smell
Chimichangas and stale cigarette smoke
Some spare change to help make it through the day
Someplace to be
Bright and early
For hopes of becoming more
Than less than nothing
A little encouragement
To think clearer
To keep hope alive
Motivation in a cup
On the road before the sun
Road leading to opportunity
Road leading away from broken dreams
Coffee, hot chocolate, swirled as one
Piping hot, straight out the tank
One sip, filling my soul with all it needed
Big smile, comfort in my hands
Happiness quantified in 10 ounces of joy and love

In my glass coffee cup
Perfectly in place
Perched on solid stone
Staring squarely at it's styrofoam friend
Layers of white and brown exposed
Feasting my eyes
My nose with its heavenly aroma
Filling me with comfort
Long before arriving to my lips
Brewed by German perfection
Right in my own home
Filtered water piped right in
Vacuum packed beans
Fresh off the boat
Foam peaking over the rim
Crystal pure cane sugar
Floating above it all
One sip before the Sun
Giving me hope for the day
Assuring me happiness in times to come
Making liquid dreams from air
Telling me I'm more than nothing
Extending sweet warmth and solace
A promise of clarity
Happiness measured out
In an 8 ounce cup of joy and love!

For the Record, For a Good Jewish Boy, For Bob

On a cloud came the thrill of lightnin'
………the sweet smell of rain……….
……………………………………………
Runnin' fingers along the grain
of Sarah's long neck…………..
came freedom ……
……of what the day would bring……….
Either way, it was all good……..
So a few notes were played,
 Our hearts were in tune…….
…….just in case……..
…….just in case…….
..…but most of all………..
…….just because !!

Swedish leather …….
…….maybe Spanish……
…….hell knows about these pants….
Smooth and buffed…..
………………..loud and soft
Days once lived…….
……….days to be lived…
Nostalgic and present…….
Just happy knowin' the address….
………..happy if the the phone starts ringin'…..
So ready to sink into the day…….
…….let the day sink into me…..
IT was all good………

.........and Sarah..............
........Sarah never sounded so fine......

IT was just another day.....
.......day after last.....
writin' a new story for the annals ......
A workin' heart.........
........like workin' hands
Rough and worn from busin' tables
........washin' dishes.....
Lotsa meanin' to be lived.....
.........jottin' notes along the way......
Got my walkin' boots on......
........'cause walkin' ....
.....always feels so good....
From here...to there........
.......to everywhere.......
Coast of California...........
......Streets of Barcelona....
The better the shoes...........
........the better the day.....
But first a phone call to be made........
Just to be........
How to be...............
Who's it gonna be???????
And man.......
I can smell the leather in my boots.......
And they ain't ever smelled so good
Just like those Eastern Trains......
.....Western Rains......

So here we are..........
Just gonna be, who we gonna be.......
Listenin' to the wind.......
Listenin' to the notes between us.....
Ain't nothin' ever sounded so good.......
'Cause we both know.......

How to be…….
Who we gonna be………
………
And man……..
……does Sarah ever sound sweet…..

Five More Minutes

Sit beside me in the moonlight
Let me hear your voice
Let me watch your hair
Pick up blue and silver rays of light
Please tell me who you are
Who you were
Who you want to be

Let us dangle our feet in the river
Listening to the rushing water
Sit with me on the soft grass
Please tell me how it feels to you
Can you smell the color green
Is the moisture coating your skin

Lie beside me on the flat rocks
Sun with me like a lizard
Feel the warmth penetrate your everything
Is the sky as blue as you have seen
Do you want to take off your soft jeans
Do you want to cover yourself in leaves

Let us listen to the city night
Can you hear the music just like me
Do the scents make you feel at home
Or are you afraid of what you cannot see
Do you like the way the night speaks
to all that we can be

Wrap yourself in my blanket
Listen to us breath
Does my hair smell like the smokey night

Would you like to touch my hand
Or is it simply enough to lie
Beside each other in this flat

Travel across the land with me
Do you feel the road move beneath our seat
Can you hear the pavement speaking back to us
May I rest my head gently upon your chest
Is my pain seeping onto your skin
Does my joy make it deep within

Can you tell the comfort your presence brings

Will you walk me to my fate
Share a scone with me
Do you like your coffee hot
You don't need to say goodbye
And yes, It's ok to dry our cries

Will you stay with me
Will you hold me tight
I know you can't let go
I see your tears
They match mine

Please stay with me
Make me laugh again
Let me wipe your eyes

One more hug my friend
Walk with me again

Please, just five more minutes

Just five more minutes

Five more minutes

Just five

Under the same light

I sit quietly under the roof of generations past
I watch with all my senses on task
History is being painted for me
Under the sun with autumn breeze
With the humming of sisters in the light
Archived emotion deeply etched on their skin
So beautiful and radiant still
It is a tally of everything kept inside
Illuminated in the light of sisterhood
Oh yes, I see it all so clear
It brings tears to my eyes
In witness of the bench
Wood carved out for little girls
To take their seat
And so they sit,
They laugh, they cry
For all the years gone by
Curtains drawn
White weathered lace
Filters the outside in
Painting gentle shadows upon their face
The scent of childhood
Drifts in with laughter and strife
Tears and sweat
Baked on a summers day
I see these girls
They walked, they jumped, they danced
Their feet and worn out shoes
They grew so much
All upon the same floor

I hear the songs of their hearts
Being played out for me
It's the sound of holding hands
Playful eyes and tugging hair
Their blood runs thick
The nectar of thieves
Stealing happiness
On the petals of spring
They were not the same
Not in the least
But they shared it all
Under the same light
Darkness softens the night
The smell of candle light, and burning oil
Enters the room with sweet remembrance
Everything has changed
From the days of youth
There is such clarity, such beauty
Such immense love
Hand crafted in sisterhood
Sitting on the same bench
All under the same light

Hannah (for Norman)

Dear Hannah,
It's been such a long time since I've seen your face
Your blue eyes in the kitchen, talking about love
like you always would, but never mentioning the past

Hannah, even your dress seemed to whisper me Love
when the world outside went cold
when tears drifted in, from the bitter streets below,

And when my body bled, my face would smile for you
just to see you look my way,
and you always did look, straight into the best part of me
then I could see me too,

Oh Hannah, how did you stay so beautiful?
I could not understand
Your own mother left standing by the water,
and all the ones with no escape, they seemed to fade
even their names, you drowned in the ocean as we crossed,

But my Hannah, you still smiled and brushed your hair
so it could glisten for me and give me beauty under the light,

And when my tears would fall, you shut the door behind me
locking out all the noise, slipping me paper under the door
just so you could read my words, and open up my world

Oh Hannah, my Ima I missed you all the days of my life
and my days went long, longer than you would ever believe
And now I'm hoping that there is a God, the one I thought was dead
just so I could see your face once more

Atalaya sunrise

New Mexico skies called me home,
into the arms of the mountain that is me.
To her body of trees and rocks,
I am urged out of bed and into the dark.
In quickened pace,
I prepare for Sun's embrace.
My legs burn for the summit,
with lungs drinking from the trees.
My mind becomes silent as to see,
all which awaits me on my perch.
It is the four directions of the wind.
Within my heart,
I anticipate my arrival to the place
where I always belong.
I am inevitably greeted
by a keeper of the mountain;
one of many creatures of earth or sky.
For today it was a bee
emerging from the dark,
rising to her presence.
She ushers me with her hum,
through castles of boulders,
corridors of trees,
till sweet twilight
showed her face to me.
And together,
we are welcomed
to our place in the sun!

Unabridged

Laughter flooded my car as I drove in solitude
I recognized part of my internal make-up
This foolish adult who dives into the silliest of ideas
Just because I can become so infatuated with life

This time it wasn't me who gave me a belly laugh
It was Dad and his love of bacon
And pork chops, and chicharrones and pork chile
So I reminisced……….

In the seventies, Dad quit his job,
Putting it all on the line for the hogs
He convinced his banker to give him a loan
To start his very own Hog farm
Who does this, the world exclaimed!
And I laughed with the greatest of joy

So the pig pen was built
And for the first time I witnessed a quality
That embodied a zest for life
And for the first time
I understood what it was to get carried away
And for the first time
I understood what it was to have life
……………..and to be life

So one day the little piggies arrived
Pink and adorable eating machines
They eventually ate us out of all our savings
Till finally Dad sent the remaining group off to market
Keeping one to fill our freezer of course

Dad shook his head, but I could see his eyes
Still glimmering with amusement
At the time he was a hog farmer for a couple of years

I now understand this so well
And how important it is for some of us
To get carried away
To throw ourselves into personal endeavors
That no one might ever understand

This is when Dad was at his best
This is when his heart radiated out
What a great gift
When humans allow themselves to be themselves
Allow themselves to fall and to fail
To be foolish and unabridged

Love and Alcohol

When you love something
You cannot abuse it
Nor squander it on petty things
I do not want to abuse alcohol
For I enjoy it way too much
I even write poetry
about it!
……..
…..
….
..

Ode to Hakkaisan Kijoshu (Sake) A Celestial Wedding of Sorts

Have a sip
Sweetness upon your lips
Lingering, tantalizing in your mouth
Pleasure is my persuasion
Sweet illusions brought to life
Dancing inside me
Like a wedding dance of sorts
Where two are joined with exquisite motion
Hand upon her back
Leading her deliberately
To the sway of the night
With sweet fragrance in the air
The cake is sliced
Cut through many layers
Liberating the complexity
Lying beneath the smooth exterior
White as the purest snow
Sweet and decadent
Layered berries
Swirls and curves
Bursting with flavor
Softness fills them up
Thick and luscious
She lifts to his call
Intertwining with all senses
Persuaded

Waltz

I know you
I have seen you before
We once danced a waltz
in the grand courtyard
under a starry sky

The air smelled of sweet blossoms in the spring
Our skin was moist from the ocean breeze
We danced to the subtle push and pull
of the music drifting in

From our delicate touch
was the loveliest song being made
as we brushed past each other so softly

Poetry, like poetry of hearts
as they pass each other in haste
and reconvene in isolated suspensions of time

The poetry of life,
breathed into me from without
I take it in fully with all that I am

I was made to be parts of others,
I was made to shape shift in the night
....
I do delight in the textures of the unknown

Letters

I love and cherish all the letters that I've written
All the letters that I've read
I don't know what I paid for these
Or which were free
But they are worth all the money in the world to me
Just to have the remembrance in my heart
Of reading words that made me exalt in joy, or sad with tears
Correspondence to and fro
Warming my insides and telling me so much
I don't think it's been their intention
To make me feel so special and alive
But they did, and they do
The words from an outside source
They make me feel like I am real
And perhaps worthy of effort back to me
You see, when someone takes the time
To tell you something that is important to them
It makes you feel important in ways that give life
And when someone writes it to you
It's like a permanent inscription on your soul
That says you were indeed here
And that someone saw you

Simple Moments

Do you ever miss a time, a place, a feeling, a person
Someone, something that made a moment worth missing
Did you memorize it unintentionally through sheer enjoyment
You sat back and just felt it, felt all the moment had to offer
You didn't mean for your cells to memorize it
But you felt it on your skin with the temperature of the air
You smelled it when you took in a deep breath of sweetness
You heard it when you were listening and didn't want to miss a thing
The intonation of a voice, its cadence its beautiful sound
And then the words that you heard
Oh how perfectly they enveloped you in sheer joy
You tasted it when you took a drink of coffee and just absorbed
What it was to feel good with the warmth entering your body
Some moments in life are brimming with sincerity and truth
And in those moments there is such clarity
And all you have to do is be present
And take notice and enjoyment in what your are experiencing
I don't mean to collect these and live in the past
But they do live in my bones and mostly in my heart

Meadowlake Street

I found myself watching you
Sauntering through an orchard beneath the trees
Hand in hand with your dreams
I could see your smile and your heart

You were holding so much beauty in your hands
Tangled up with the deepest parts of you

She really did take your breath away.............

I felt it as I noticed how the light played on her skin
Shadows entwined with the effortless contours of her form

Browns, reds and yellows leading me to visions of autumn
Where I am suddenly surrounded by a flood of memories
Moments once captured with such intensity
Now encapsulated in the warm, soft glow of dying embers

Already nostalgic, sadness floods my heart
I can see the light slowly dissipating
The colors steadily changing with time

Her skin, soft and warm to the touch persists on mine
And in the silence, I am taken by her flavor
She lingers on my lips like my sweetest memories

This dream is now coming to it's end
I feel the rug being pulled out from under me
It's magic now gone

My tears fall with the same certainty
That my heart felt the depths of her soul

And as she begins to disappear
This love remains suspended in eternity
Where it belongs as something
Which multiplied my heart
For those who awaited my arrival

I Am Life

You didn't think you would see her again
Well you're seeing her right now
Here she is, erupting into flames
She is the fire that burns in your heart
When you feel more than you can think
When life explodes,
She seeps out from the grain on the wood
Wanting to be set free from the rings of time that bound her in
She has always been inside, trying to push herself out
To be seen
To be known
To be loved

Like a rosebush,
She hurts
She loves
She knows the difference between life and death
And she appreciates them both
She longs for them both
Lighting herself on fire for them equally
She knows no beginnings, she knows no ends
Just right now
What's in front of you

Look at her
Can you hear her?
This is how she sounds
You can listen to her soul
If you just study the lines on her face,
You can taste her,
If you just follow her curves into the unknown

All her softness is right there
It's encased by fire and thorns
All her benevolence is there,
It's shrouded with all thats sharp and bold

Look closely and you will see her
In all her beauty

She is joy, like the wings of a dragon fly
Taking you to far away lands
Where the sky is purple
And the earth is blue
Where love reigns true

She is you

Lake Powell in Early Spring

He parked the red Dakota on the mesa,

Door swung ajar
I ran to the edge
Down the clay I slid
Watching red being diluted to
Washed out pink
Finally, touching the emerald jewel at my feet
Scanning into the sapphire of the deep
Nike Pegasus traded for transforming my toes to fins

No people in sight
My pants were next, till I was all fish
I felt the texture of the smooth clay beneath the water
Shockingly cold and glistening in the sun

I had the vision before it occurred
Standing on the edge
Walls of protection encircling such depth
I was taken before I arrived
No hesitation in sight

It was a move of conviction
Head first, feet last
To flow with the water
To go under
To shiver
To have the sun diminish in sight
I didn't know how deep I could go
I went in
I went down, down, down

Till I remembered the air I had forgot
Shooting me back to mammalian form

And when I surfaced I gulped in the sky
Now exhibiting her deepest shade of blue
With a singular puff of white

Naked in the water
Far from the arms of the cliffs
I floated on my back
Feeling my body rise and fall with each breath
Knowing this is where I belonged

Nearly ingested by lake and sky,
I could hear a voice calling out from above
Be careful……
It was too late,
All caution already handed to the wind
I felt as a safe as I could ever be

Embraced fully by the water
Held in such love
I sank my head down till my ears were under
My face covered
Nostrils narrowly peaking out
Shivers expunged

……..and the world was coming to standstill
Barely moving my legs
The voice from beyond became muffled
I could no longer make out the words
Making me singular and fluid
Alone even amongst any crowd

I no longer cared about body image
Unified with the water, carefree as she
Spectators were now free
If some stranger was to come and slit my throat,
It mattered not

No,
I didn't care
Because this moment was perfect
So worth life
It was brilliant
It tingled with immortality
Persisting
Infinitely

Side by Side

My love will accompany you even when I'm not there

When you search the room for me wondering where I could be,

My love is under the very same roof

When we live our separate lives, or death has us parted,

My love will be in the air that you breath

When we walk side by side, along our separate paths,

Across the continent, across lifetimes,

Right at your side is oodles and oodles of my love

Fire

Snow falls silently to the ground
Crystal ice inside her window
Eyes open before daybreak
Craving warmth,
Needing to ignite the fire

Fleece lined denim jacket over pajamas
Daddy's boots up to her knees
Attentive not to tumble down the stairs

Never flipping a switch for sight
Instead, hunting outside in darkness
Ocotito, juniper, pinion, dry pine

Sunday's Rio Grande Sun by flashlight
Separating ads
Front page crime,
Perfect for a clean burn

Kerosene on the windowsill, for amateurs, not I
Only the art of crumpled paper, sticks, separation, togetherness,
Special specimens deliberately selected
To arouse a flaming teepee

One match,
Struck,
Watching words quickly turn to glowing ash
Dancing flames
Igniting pitch
Blazing sticks

Fiery Pine
Then goes the pinion, full combustion!

Crackling,
Mesmerized by the colors
Blue, yellow, orange, red
Like a Rainbow in the Dark
Fervently painting her skin

Owning this sliver of time,
No one yet awake
She slips back to cold sheets
Back to dreams
Only to wake again
This time to warmth
Like it had always been there

Light peeks through the window
The smell of bacon sizzling
Dio playing in the kitchen
Holy Diver,
Her brother makes her eggs to perfection
Crispy around the edges,
Yolky on the inside,
A dash of salt, pepper too
Served up on a pretty plate,
As if she was the princess
Like Mom might do if she was to wake

Of Runners Times

Trees applaud my effort with their dying leaves,
…………..panting up the hill,
shoes laced tight……..

I hear them cheering as a crowd at the bullfight,
…………..echoing from the arena outside its walls,
on cobblestone streets below……….

Light clipped to my pocket,
on the inside,
……only moon shines bright

     My heart cries of empty spaces,
trying to fill…….

Yet, I am champion to those with no legs,
….. clapping in the breeze

My lungs are strong,
………..only momentarily breathless,
till I descend to rising sun……..

I expire the residue of what ails me,
…………..a remedy concocted in the dark,
in the laboratory of my synapses

…………………………and I hear the applause,
You flatter me dear leaves!

A Grain of Sand

Getting lost in the metaphors
is sometimes all we need
It's the way to heighten
and hold on to a feeling,
encapsulate it forever
Simple words that define
are never close to how it feels
This is why
it all falls down
like a grain of sand
The hourglass
is always so much more
than just time

Diagnosis

A new chapter
Slamming the door on my fingers
Cutting them off at the tips

A torch lights fire to my clothing
......only I'm still wearing it!!!!!!
Undressing as fast as I can,
I'm naked in public

I smell my hair burn
Watching the plume of smoke surround me

People throw buckets of water in my direction
Not wanting me to disintegrate right before their eyes

But the only cure is more fire
Burn me alive

WOW , I'm in shock
Simply in shock

And already hurting

Decay

Uneasy,
Only clouds drifting in my head
Like a fog putting me to sleep
It must be the drugs
Pumping through my veins
Trying to take me away
Just as I was finally ready to live

Dead man walking
What a thing to be told

I have a purpose
I've found meaning
I'm starting to see it

No time to waste
Maybe just days
Or weeks
Or years

Expiration unknown
With a short shelf life I'm told

I'm Perishable
I will expire
So will you
It's true

My dog can smell it
The volatile smell of decay
It's real..

How did I ever forget!!

About the Author

Melina was raised by her parents, three older brothers and several furry companions in the arroyos, mountains and streams of the Sangre de Cristo Mountains near Taos, New Mexico.

Melina attended New Mexico State University, however after meeting some hardship, dropped out to join the family business of crushing automobiles and recycling scrap iron. Melina took her role in the business traveling New Mexico, Arizona, Colorado and vast areas of the Native Reservations collecting diverse experiences and skills.

After working for her family, Melina went on to live in Los Lunas, NM, Winterhaven, CA, Beaty, NV and landed in Las Vegas, Nevada where she lived for over 20 years. During this time she worked many jobs ranging from Spanish radio trivia host, blueprint editor, prep cook, exotic dancer, secretary, Rainbow Vacuum sales person and writing fuels contracts for a large power company amongst other things.

When given the chance Melina went back to the University of Nevada, Las Vegas to study biology, physics and continued on to earn her Doctorate of Dental Medicine at UNLV School of Dental Medicine.

In 2015 Melina, her husband and companion of over 32 years and children moved to Santa Fe, NM where she now owns and operates a successful Dental Practice. Currently she spends her days enjoying her family, career, running, hiking and enjoying the arts, especially writing. She is now working on her second book which will be dedicated to those affected by cancer.

FLOWERSONG
PRESS

FlowerSong Press nurtures essential verse
from, about, and throughout the borderlands.
Literary. Lyrical. Boundless.

Sign up for announcements about
new and upcoming titles at:

www.flowersongpress.com

www.ingramcontent.com/pod-product-compliance
Lightning Source LLC
Chambersburg PA
CBHW051312120626
46547CB00015B/2206